The
UFO
Challenge

The UFO Challenge

by Richard Michael Rasmussen

LUCENT
B·O·O·K·S

Look for these and other books in the Lucent Overview series:

Acid Rain
AIDS
Animal Rights
The Beginning of Writing
Dealing with Death
Drug Trafficking
Drugs and Sports
Endangered Species

Energy Alternatives
Garbage
Homeless Children
Smoking
Special Effects in the Movies
Teen Alcoholism
The UFO Challenge
Vietnam

Library of Congress Cataloging-in-Publication Data

Rasmussen, Richard Michael.
    The UFO Challenge / by Richard Michael Rasmussen.
      p. cm. — (Lucent overview series)
    Includes bibliographical references (p. 124).
    Summary: Examines incidents involving reported sightings of unidentified flying objects and meetings with aliens, describes how people react in these situations, and discusses how the authorities are investigating.
    ISBN 1-56006-104-9
    1. Unidentified flying objects—Juvenile literature.
    [1. Unidentified flying objects.] I. Title. II. Series.
TL789.R36 1990
001.9'42—dc20
                                           90-32962
                                               CIP
                                               AC

16604358

© Copyright 1990 by Lucent Books, Inc.
P.O. Box 289011, San Diego, CA 92128-9011

Contents

Introduction

ON THE EVENING of November 15, 1974, a bright, white sphere of light appeared over a farm near Ramona, California. Ten witnesses—eight children and two adults—watched the object for hours. It hovered in the sky and caused extraordinary incidents to occur on the ground. Crazy zigzag patterns appeared on a television set inside the farmhouse. Static noise crackled over the radio. A compass needle spun wildly during the sighting. Cats, dogs, chickens, goats, and horses became restless. Inside the farmhouse a cat even ran into a wall several times, trying to escape.

An even stranger event occurred on August 21, 1955, near Kelly, Kentucky, at about 7:00 P.M. As teenager Billy Ray Sutton stepped outside the family farmhouse, he saw a huge, bright object landing in the distance. He ran back inside to report his sighting, but no one paid attention.

An hour later, however, a barking dog alerted the family that something was wrong. Approaching the farmhouse was a glowing creature, under four feet tall, with long arms, a rounded head, and pointed ears. When it was only twenty feet away, two adults fired at it. The creature somersaulted and scrambled off into the darkness.

Then a second creature peered through a window screen into the house. A shot was fired, and the

Swiss caretaker Eduard Meier shot this photograph of an apparent alien ship. Meier claims that he was contacted by a friendly alien race in 1975.

creature, apparently wounded, ran away. As one of the adults went outside to find the creature, a claw-like hand reached down from the roof to grab him. Another creature was perched on a tree branch, watching. Shots were fired at both creatures, but this time the bullets seemed to bounce off their bodies.

The frightened family locked itself inside the house. From time to time, the creatures appeared at their windows, looking in with round, glowing, yellow eyes. Finally, at about 11:00 P.M., the family dashed for the car and raced into town to the police station. City, county, and state police rushed to the scene, only to find nothing but evidence of a shootout. The strange craft and its occupants had mysteriously disappeared.

Across the country, and indeed around the world, people report similar sightings of unidentified flying

An artist's depiction of an alien and spaceship.

objects (UFOs) and associated creatures. UFOs are objects or lights in the sky or on the ground that remain unidentified after sufficient study and investigation.

Some reports of UFO sightings are hoaxes. They are stories made up by the witnesses for various self-serving reasons. Perhaps these people want attention, or maybe they hope to make money by writing a book.

Most of the people reporting UFOs, however, are honest and reliable. Many are professionals and have jobs as police officers, fire fighters, military officers, news reporters, airline pilots, and teachers, for example. All these people have one thing in common—they have seen something they cannot explain.

Over the years, these witnesses have filed hundreds of thousands of UFO reports. After sufficient investigation 90 to 95 percent of the cases are explained. Most are due to human-made phenomena, such as satellites and weather balloons. Others are due to natural phenomena, such as meteors (superheated rocks falling toward earth from outer space). However, about 5 to 10 percent of the reports remain unexplained. These, the unidentified cases, are the true UFOs: cases that baffle our minds, intrigue our curiosity, stimulate our imaginations, and touch our sense of wonder. They challenge our very ability to identify them.

Ufologists, those people who investigate and study UFO reports, are trying to solve the mystery. So are a small number of scientists. But so far, despite many government, military, and private investigations, no one has yet satisfactorily explained the existence of UFOs.

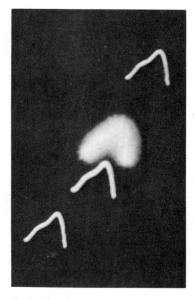

In 1973, photographer Ken Chamberlain Jr. shot this picture of strange lights in the sky over Columbus, Ohio.

1

The Early UFOs: Mysterious Airships, Foo Fighters, and Ghost Rockets

This photo, taken in 1951 by George Adamski, purportedly shows a large "mother ship" releasing several "flying saucers."

THE DRONING OF enormous engines sung down from the dark, cloudy heavens. A brilliant beam of light shone through the evening mist to the ground. The beam illuminated the neighborhood with an eerie glow. Inside one house, a young girl noticed the glow through her living room window. Thinking that there was a fire outside, she ran outdoors to warn the neighbors.

As she ran out onto the front lawn, the girl saw the beam of light. She looked upward, following the beam of light, to a strange, shadowy object moving silently, like an apparition, through the mist. The object was cigar-shaped, with four large wings extending from a metallic body. Gigantic fanlike propellers drove the object along, against the wind. The craft swayed slightly as it moved.

An artist's version of the ship that supposedly passed over Sacramento, Oakland, and San Francisco in 1896. Witnesses claimed they heard singing voices emanating from the ship.

As the object moved on, the beam of light continued to sweep the ground, much in the manner of a searchlight. Other residents ran into their yards, pointing and shouting in excitement at the sight of the mysterious object.

For more than thirty minutes, the object hovered over the city of Sacramento, California. During this time, it generated dozens of reports, including one filed by the mayor's daughter.

Strangely, many citizens heard odd sounds coming from the object. One witness, F. Wenzel of Scheld's Brewery, said that he heard a "merry chorus" drifting down from the vessel. Another, T.P. Long, told reporters, "I could hear the voices of the occupants singing, and it sounded to me like the noise produced by a phonograph."

Employees of the Sacramento Streetcar Company reported seeing the craft. They also heard "a rattling song" overhead. One, foreman G.C. Snyder, said that the object was "laboring as a seagoing vessel will in a heavy sea and head wind." Another, motorman F.E. Brigs, stopped his streetcar as the airship passed overhead. Passengers leaped out in time to see the object and hear the sounds of voices and singing.

One witness reported that the object drifted downward, dangerously close to housetops. A voice from the craft reportedly said, in perfect English, "Lift her up, quick. You are making directly for that steeple."

Eventually, the vessel headed off toward the southwest and mysteriously disappeared from view.

The next day, the headlines of the *San Francisco Call* reported the story:

CLAIM THEY SAW A FLYING SHIP
Strange Tale of Sacramento Men. . .
Viewed an Aerial Courser as It Passed Over
the City at Night
Declare They Heard
Voices of Those Aboard Join in Merry Chorus

The most amazing thing about this sighting is that it occurred on the evening of September 17, 1896. This was at a time when flying craft of this sort did not yet exist in the United States.

A great wave of sightings

The event marked the beginning of a large "flap"—a wave of sightings—that would spread from Sacramento to San Francisco. It would then move on to other parts of California and eventually across the nation and to parts of Canada. It would continue until May of 1897, leaving in its path a legacy of strange sightings and events that are still largely unexplained.

Comparison of various old newspaper accounts reveals differing descriptions of the airship, including the phrases "dark body," "cigar-shaped," "barrel-shaped," "misty mass," "egg-shaped," "slow," and "fast." This suggests that more than one craft was involved during the course of the flap. Indeed, one witness, newspaper editor Frank Dickson, could scarcely believe his eyes when he saw two airships at once. He said that they were "four hundred feet apart" and "communicating with each other by means of red and green lights."

Airship occupants

Among the most interesting airship cases are those involving reported sightings of airship occupants and of actual contacts between witnesses and the occupants. On April 15, 1897, airship witnesses in Belle Plaine, Iowa, saw "two queer looking persons on board, who made desperate efforts to conceal themselves." In 1896, the *San Francisco Call* told the story of a witness in the woods who came across six beings, human in appearance, building an airship on the ground. The beings asked the witness to keep the discovery a secret, but the witness felt

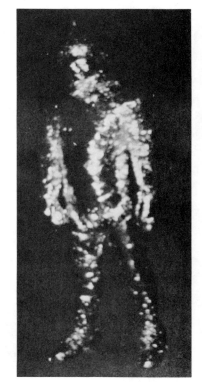

On October 18, 1973, a policeman in Falkville, Alabama took this picture of a mysterious-looking creature.

obligated to tell his story when airship accounts made the news. In 1897, witnesses in Chattanooga, Tennessee, described a "vessel resting on a spur of a mountain near this city. Two men were at work on it and explained that they had been compelled to return to earth because the machinery was out of order."

The Alexander Hamilton contact case

A contact case making big headlines involved Alexander Hamilton of Leroy, Kansas. On April 19, 1897, Hamilton went outside with his son and a tenant to see, in Hamilton's words, "an airship slowly descending over my cow lot about forty rods from the house." The three-hundred-foot craft was cigar-shaped, with a passenger section underneath, much like a modern blimp.

A cable stretched from the airship down to the ground. The other end of the cable was fastened to a calf that was caught in a fence. As the craft descended, Hamilton noticed "six of the strangest beings I ever saw" inside the craft, who were "jabber-

Does this image represent a UFO, or is it a trick played by nature?

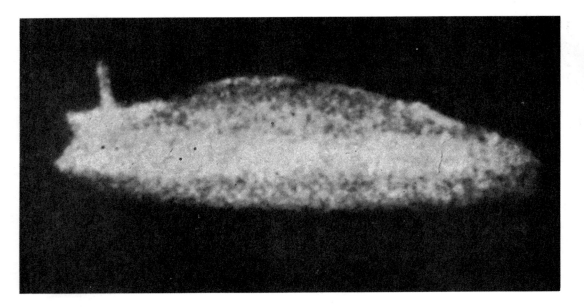

ing" in a strange language. The witnesses tried to free the calf from the fence, but they could not. So they cut away the fence section instead. They "stood in amazement to see ship, cow and all rise slowly and take off."

When Hamilton's astonishing story appeared in the *Farmer's Advocate*, it generated much excitement. But some people thought right away that it was a hoax, even though the witnesses made sworn statements that the story was true.

Ships from other worlds?

Many newspapers carried editorials saying the sightings were due to hallucinations (imagined events that did not really happen), hoaxes, or heavy drinking. Many others explained them as the work of secret inventors. Some newspapers, however, speculated that the craft were extraterrestrial, or from other worlds. The *St. Louis Post-Dispatch* said that "these may be visitors from Mars, fearful, at the last, of invading the planet they have been seeking." The *Washington Times* suggested that Martians were exploring our planet. This speculation about extraterrestrial visitation provides an interesting link between the airship sightings of the last century and the UFO reports of today.

As with modern sightings, many of the early airship accounts can be explained as exaggerated stories or natural phenomena, such as clouds, meteors, or tricks of the atmosphere. Determining the facts after so much time is difficult. Most researchers, however, are convinced that of the approximately one thousand airship sightings on record, about two hundred are unexplainable. As such, these sightings qualify as legitimate UFOs.

After May of 1897, the great flap ended. Over the years, people forgot about the sightings. The stories faded from memory until modern-day researchers,

Many researchers claim that UFO sightings can be explained by natural phenomena, such as this unusual cloud formation in Marseilles, France.

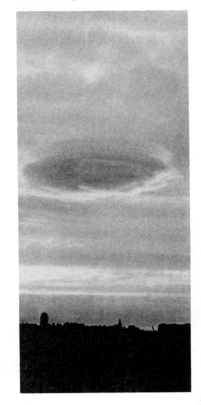

looking for examples of early UFOs, rediscovered the old newspaper accounts.

The mysterious foo fighters

The next great series of sightings did not happen until the last year of World War II. At that time, U.S. bomber pilots over Germany and Japan began seeing strange objects—fiery balls of light and glowing disk-shaped objects—flying alongside or behind their aircraft.

One such case occurred on the night of November 23, 1944, when a B-29 bomber piloted by Lt. Ed Schlueter patrolled the hazardous skies over Germany's Rhine River. Intelligence officer Lt. Fred Ringwald, on board as an observer, was the first to spot what seemed to be stars in the distance. As the objects approached, the crew became excited. They could now see that the objects were actually eight to ten orange balls of light "moving through the air at a terrific speed." The lights zoomed off and soon vanished from sight. The puzzling objects were not detected by radar equipment, either from the ground or on board the bomber.

Charles Odom, a B-17 pilot from 1944 to 1945, recalled his experiences with the strange objects in a 1947 interview with reporters: "They looked like crystal balls, clear, about the size of basketballs." They would approach the aircraft, "then would seem to become magnetized to our formation and fly alongside. They never came closer than three hundred feet. After a while, they would peel off like a plane and leave."

The objects became known as "foo fighters," even though they never once fought. The name apparently came from a *Smokey Stover* comic strip that made a joke about the French word *feu*, which means fire. The cartoon contained a line that said, "Where there's foo, there's fire." The objects were also called "foo balls" and "fireball fighters."

Most foo fighters ranged in size from one to five feet in diameter. They flew alone, in pairs, or in small groups. Often they changed color while in flight. Sometimes they "teased" pilots by speeding up or slowing down or by dodging airplanes when they approached. Such behavior suggested that the objects might be under intelligent control.

At first the pilots were alarmed by the foo fighters, fearing that they were some kind of new enemy weapon. But it soon became obvious that the objects were harmless. Military personnel then speculated that the foo fighters were some kind of "psychological weapon" meant to confuse and frighten Allied pilots. This theory was popular until postwar examination of German and Japanese records failed to find any evidence to support it. The theory was weakened further when the Allies discovered that German and Japanese pilots had also encountered the foo fighters during similar flying missions. Some ufologists have therefore concluded that the foo fighters were extraterrestrial probes, robotlike craft sent here from other worlds to monitor the war.

After the war, the foo fighter sightings stopped.

During World War II, U.S. bomber pilots reported seeing glowing objects zooming alongside their planes. Dubbed "foo fighters," these strange but harmless objects were never explained.

Before long, however, a new kind of sighting took place, this time in Scandinavian countries.

The ghost rockets of 1946

It was the night of June 9, 1946, when a British reporter in Helsinki, Finland, saw an astonishing sight in the darkened skies. A cigar-shaped object sped rapidly overhead, spewing a tremendous trail of fire and smoke in its wake. Even after the object disappeared from view, the air along its flight path glowed. The reporter was unable to make sense out of what he saw.

A short while later, frightened witnesses on the Finnish coast saw a similar object racing toward them from the Baltic Sea. As they dashed for cover, the object suddenly changed directions and headed back to sea.

Hearing of the second report, the reporter in Helsinki realized that a big story was in the works. He wired the news to his paper, the *Daily Mail* in London. The sensational story soon attracted international attention.

As weeks and months went by, more and more reports came in. "Silver torpedo," "cylinderlike," "luminous bodies," "bullet-shaped," "silvery projectile," "rocketlike," and "missilelike" were common descriptions. The mysterious nature of the objects led newspapers to dub them "ghost rockets."

Sometimes, the objects exploded in flight, scattering material into the air. Recovery of dark, tiny, burnt fragments on the ground convinced some investigators that the objects were meteors. But numerous observations seemed to refute this explanation. According to witnesses, the objects often flew parallel to the ground, or dived and then climbed, or reversed direction in flight, all things that meteors do not do.

Many authorities feared that the ghost rockets

Is this cigar-shaped formation an alien ship or can it be explained by natural or man-made occurrences?

were the result of secret rocket experiments by the Soviet Union. Sweden, in particular, supported this explanation. Many newspapers published anti-Soviet editorials, accusing the Soviets of "bombarding" Swedish skies. Beginning in late July, the Swedish government barred newspapers from printing the locations of ghost rocket sightings. Within days, the Norwegian and Danish governments passed similar laws. And on August 31, the government of Norway totally banned newspapers from reporting ghost rocket information. All along, however, the Soviet Union denied any responsibility for the ghost rockets.

In October, the Swedish defense ministry issued a press release declaring that about eight hundred of the one thousand ghost rocket reports were explainable as natural or human-made phenomena. The release admitted, however, that radar had detected some two hundred objects "which cannot be the phenomena of nature or products of imagination, nor can they be referred to as Swedish airplanes." Details of the full investigation were never released.

Other than brief recurrences in 1948, the ghost rocket sightings vanished. Their origin is still a mystery today.

Even though the terms *UFO* and *flying saucer* had not yet been coined, the ghost rockets of 1946 represented the first major flap of the twentieth century. As exciting as these sightings were, however, they would pale against the events to come in the United States starting in June of 1947.

2

The Flying Saucer Era: Silvery Disks, Crashed Saucers, and UFOs over the White House

THE SINGLE-ENGINE airplane came to a screeching halt on the runway at the Pendleton, Oregon airport, late in the afternoon of June 24, 1947. As pilot Kenneth Arnold climbed out of the cockpit, he was greeted by an eager crowd of reporters and airport personnel. They wanted to hear his amazing story firsthand.

Surprised by the waiting crowd, Arnold spoke reluctantly. It had happened earlier in the day, he said, while flying near Mt. Rainier. He had been on the way to Yakima, Washington, searching for a downed C-46 marine transport plane.

Arnold said, "It was during this search . . . at approximately 9,200 feet altitude, that a tremendously bright flash lit up the surfaces of my aircraft. I was startled . . . I spent the next twenty to thirty seconds

Pilot Kenneth Arnold looks skyward. In 1947, Arnold sighted a group of mysterious disc-shaped objects while flying a plane over the Cascade Mountains in Washington.

urgently searching the sky all round, in an attempt to determine where the flash of light had come from."

Arnold explained that before he had time to collect his thoughts, the flash happened again. This time he noticed the direction. What he saw caught him by surprise. "I observed, far to my left and to the north, a formation of very bright objects, flying very close to the mountaintops and traveling at tremendous speed."

Mysterious shapes

At first he could not identify the shapes. "I watched as these objects rapidly neared the snow border of Mt. Rainier . . . in group count, they numbered nine. They were flying diagonally in formation with a large gap between the first four and the last five. What startled me at this point was the fact that I could not find any tails on them." As Arnold drew closer, he could see more detail. They looked, he said, "flat like a pie pan and so shiny they reflected the sun like a mirror."

Arnold watched in awe as the objects flew behind and between the jagged peaks of the Cascade Mountains. From this observation, he was able to calculate the distance of the objects and figure their air speed. He estimated their speed to be between 1,300 to 1,700 miles per hour. The fastest jets, he noted, reached speeds of only 700 miles per hour.

After the objects disappeared from view, Arnold flew on to Yakima, where he mentioned his experience to airport workers. He then took off for Pendleton, only to find that word of his sighting had arrived ahead of him, along with the crowd of reporters.

As he talked to the reporters, Arnold recalled, "Another characteristic of these craft that made a tremendous impression on me was how they flut-

Arnold, who claims he saw a fluttering object such as this, coined the term "flying saucer."

tered and sailed, tipping their wings alternately and emitting those very bright blue-white flashes from their surfaces. . . . Their flight was like speedboats on rough water. . . . They flew like a saucer would if you skipped it across the water."

The reporters, originally skeptical, were so impressed with Arnold's account that they raced to the phones to file their reports. Overnight, sensational stories of Arnold's "flying pie pans" and "flying saucers" hit the news wires. *Flying saucers* rapidly became a household word, and before long, people all across the country were reporting strange objects in the skies. Suddenly, and quite unexpectedly, the "Flying Saucer Era" was well underway.

The Mantell crash

Nearly six months later, on January 7, 1948, an event occurred that frightened people throughout the United States. Flight controllers at Godman Air Force Base near Louisville, Kentucky, received reports of a strange, silvery, cone-shaped object in the sky. The controllers ran outdoors and saw the object themselves. After deciding it was not an aircraft or weather balloon, they radioed the sighting to some Air National Guard planes flying overhead. One plane, piloted by Capt. Thomas Mantell, pursued the UFO.

As Mantell approached the object, it zoomed off suddenly and climbed higher. Mantell reported, "I see something above and ahead of me, and I'm still climbing." Controllers asked him to describe the object. Mantell said, "It looks metallic in appearance and is tremendous in size."

Anxious to identify the object further, Mantell continued the chase. He reported, "It's above me, and I'm gaining on it. I'm going to twenty thousand feet."

Those were the last words ever heard from

In 1948, while flying an Air National Guard plane, Capt. Thomas Mantell pursued an unidentified cone-shaped object. During the chase, Mantell's plane went into a nosedive and exploded, killing him and frightening the public.

The shocked public feared that Mantell's plane had been attacked by an alien ship, such as the one depicted here.

Mantell. The flight controllers abruptly lost contact with him. Hours later, his body was found near the scattered wreckage of his crashed airplane, ninety miles from Godman Air Force Base. Reportedly, the plane had gone into a nosedive and exploded in midair. News of the chase and crash shocked the public. Many feared that Mantell was shot down by a flying saucer, perhaps a hostile vessel from outer space.

Military officials provided an explanation. They said that Mantell had mistaken the planet Venus for a UFO. As he headed upward toward the UFO, he reached an altitude of twenty thousand feet. Accordingly, he then blacked out from the lack of oxygen and lost control of his aircraft. This Venus explanation was refuted, however, when subsequent investigation revealed that the planet was not visible at the time. Was the military covering up something?

Several years later, officials said that Mantell probably died chasing a long, silvery Skyhook weather balloon, at the time a classified project unknown to Mantell or those on the ground. Skyhook launch records, however, cannot account for a balloon in Mantell's area, and the case remains unsolved.

Project Sign formed

As more people reported unusual objects in the skies, the military became worried. Afraid that UFOs might pose a security threat, the Air Force in January of 1948 formed a secret study known as

The wreckage of Mantell's plane. Officials later claimed that the unidentified object that Mantell chased was nothing more than a weather balloon.

Project Sign. The goal was to "collect, collate, evaluate and distribute to interested government agencies and contractors all information concerning sightings and phenomena in the atmosphere."

The Chiles-Whitted sighting

While military personnel organized Project Sign and began investigating reports, a sensational new sighting took place. At 2:45 A.M. on July 24, 1948, two Eastern Airlines pilots, Clarence S. Chiles and

Eastern Airlines pilots John B. Whitted and Clarence S. Chiles arm themselves with cameras and binoculars after claiming to see a wingless ship during a flight from Houston in 1948.

John B. Whitted, were flying a DC-3 passenger aircraft over Montgomery, Alabama. Suddenly, they saw a bright, cigar-shaped object heading rapidly toward them. Chiles said, "Look, here comes a new Army jet job."

When the object continued along its path, the pilots veered to avoid a collision. The object, displaying a type of antenna structure on its nose and rows of lighted windows, roared by to the right. Orange flames belched from the rear of the UFO as it climbed into the clouds at an estimated seven hundred miles per hour.

Only one passenger was awake during the episode. He noticed a bright flash as the object passed by but did not see the craft itself. The sighting was confirmed, however, by another pilot in the area. He independently reported a cigar-shaped object with orange flames.

The story appeared in newspapers nationwide. Because the pilots were trained observers with excellent reputations, most people believed that they had seen something very strange. At Project Sign, investigators were especially shaken by the sighting. It was the first time that reliable observers had encountered a UFO at close range—and survived. They classified this UFO as an "unknown"—Air Force terminology for an unexplained case.

Astronomers tried explaining the case as the sighting of a meteor, but the explanation did not account for the object zooming upward into the clouds.

In 1967, Ken Baker and Ron Forest reportedly shot this picture of a UFO over Salem, Oregon.

Secret report: UFOs are extraterrestrial craft

In its early months, Project Sign was run by people dedicated to determining the nature of UFOs. Many felt that the evidence supported the extraterrestrial explanation. Shortly after the Chiles-Whitted sighting, they produced an unofficial, top secret report called "Estimate of the Situation." It contained a startling conclusion: UFOs were from other planets. But when the report reached the desk of Air Force chief of staff Gen. Hoyt S. Vandenberg, the general rejected the report for "lack of proof." Reportedly, all copies of this report were destroyed.

Policy change

Vandenberg's skepticism over the "Estimate" paper evidently led to a policy change at Project Sign. The people who favored the extraterrestrial explanation were removed. The people who favored conventional explanations—who supported the belief that UFOs were actually clouds, stars, meteors, etc.—took charge. In December of 1948, this bias against the extraterrestrial explanation became especially apparent because the name of the study was changed to Project Grudge.

Later, in February of 1949, a final, official tech-

In 1947, Navy officials concluded that this wingless plane, called the "flying pancake," could be mistaken for a UFO. However, up to this time, the plane had never left Bridgeport, Connecticut, and sightings had occurred across the country.

nical report from Project Sign was released to authorized personnel. The report said: "No definite and conclusive evidence is yet available that would prove or disprove the existence of these unidentified objects as real aircraft of unknown and unconventional configuration." The report admitted, however, that 20 percent of the cases were unsolved and recommended further studies.

Under Project Grudge, the policy shifted from one of impartial investigation to one of explaining away as many reports as possible. Air Force officials believed UFOs were either natural or human-made phenomena. They did not want to invest a lot of time and money investigating every case. Astronomer J. Allen Hynek was hired to search for reports of UFOs that could be explained as stars, planets, and tricks of the atmosphere. Officials believed that publication of these reports would convince people that further UFO study was a waste of time. Still, even with Hynek's help, the Project Grudge team could not explain 23 percent of their cases.

Military coverup charged

Publishers at *True* magazine decided that special military connections might help in uncovering the truth about flying saucers. In late 1949, they commissioned a retired Marine Corps major, Donald E. Keyhoe, to interview key military personnel and write an article about his findings. Keyhoe, however, could not get the answers he wanted. He concluded that there was a "conspiracy of silence" at work among military officials.

Keyhoe's article, "The Flying Saucers Are Real," appeared in the January 1950 issue of *True*. It accused the Air Force of covering up the fact that flying saucers were piloted by "living, intelligent observers from another planet." This startling accusa-

Retired Marine Corps Major Donald E. Keyhoe believes that intelligent aliens pilot mysterious UFOs.

In the 1950s, UFO coverage received widespread media attention, as this 1954 magazine cover suggests.

tion, coupled with Keyhoe's image as a no-nonsense military man, made the article one of the most widely read in American publishing history. (Later in the year, the article was expanded into a full-length, best-selling paperback.)

The first American UFO book, *Behind the Flying Saucers,* by newspaper writer Frank Scully, appeared shortly after the Keyhoe article. Not only did the book accuse the Air Force of concealing the truth, it furthermore made an incredible charge that in 1948 a total of three flying saucers had crashed.

One reportedly went down near Phoenix, Arizona, and two crashed near Aztec, New Mexico. There were no survivors. Supposedly, the Air Force removed dozens of alien bodies for medical examination and dismantled the spaceships for study.

Later, an investigative reporter established that the story was a hoax, and Scully himself eventually admitted that it was fiction.

Did flying saucers actually crash?

Over the years, rumors have persisted that there actually was a crash. The rumors also say that the frozen alien bodies are to this day held by the Air Force in a secret location. One version is that the bodies are held at the Wright-Patterson Air Force

Charles Wilholm and his wife Gori believe that these photographs, taken on July 7, 1948 in Mexico, show the bodies of aliens in the wreckage of a crashed flying saucer. The photos were given to the couple by a Navy photographer.

Base in Dayton, Ohio. Another is that a crashed saucer and alien body are hidden at Langley Field, Virginia. (Ufologists sometimes refer to this as the "Hangar 18" case, in reference to an Air Force hangar where the saucer and bodies are supposedly stored. Hollywood even turned the story into a movie in 1980, *Hangar 18,* loosely based on the Scully legend.)

The inspiration for Scully's hoax may have come from an incident that occurred in Roswell, New Mexico, in July of 1948. A sheep rancher found fragments of a foil-like substance over a quarter-mile area. The *Roswell Daily Record* quoted an Army-Air Force spokesman as saying, "The many rumors regarding the flying disk became a reality yesterday when the intelligence office . . . was fortunate enough to gain possession of a disk through the cooperation of one of the local ranchers." The

In 1967, a New Mexico State University student sighted and photographed this UFO in New Mexico.

spokesman was forced to admit his error, however, when the "flying disk" turned out to be the wreckage of a weather device.

Upon close investigation, most of the continuing rumors about crashed saucers are traced back to the old Scully story. Efforts to confirm the rumors have proven fruitless.

Controversial photographs

The year 1950 was noted for more than just the Keyhoe and Scully charges, however. One of the most controversial and closely studied cases in UFO history occurred at about 7:30 A.M. on May 11, on a farm near McMinnville, Oregon. On that date, Mrs. Paul Trent stepped outdoors to see a bright, silvery disk hovering silently in the sky beyond her house. Her heart pounding, Mrs. Trent shouted for her husband. When he did not respond, she ran inside to get him. Mr. Trent grabbed a camera on the way out and quickly took two photographs of the object just before it headed off toward the northwest.

In 1950, farmer Paul Trent photographed this picture of an apparent flying saucer over his farm in McMinnvile, Oregon.

Is there a conventional explanation for this UFO sighting over the Trent's farm in Oregon? Experts disagree.

The photos show a saucer-shaped object, featuring a two-tier structure and a tail fin on top, hovering in the distance. In one picture, part of the house is in the foreground and telephone lines are in the background.

At first, the Trents showed the photos only to friends. Eventually, however, the pictures were published nationally, causing a sensation across the country.

Proof of flying saucers?

Over the years, these pictures have been looked at by dozens of experts. Astronomer William Hartmann, who examined the photos years later for the University of Colorado's scientific UFO study, was impressed. He concluded that "an extraordinary flying object, silvery, metallic, disk-shaped, tens of meters in diameter, and evidently artificial, flew within sight of two witnesses."

Investigator Robert Sheaffer, who also studied the photos, disagreed. Citing lighting differences between the two pictures and inconsistencies in the Trent's verbal account, he decided the photographs were fakes. The Trents, he charged, photographed a small model hanging from telephone lines. As evidence, he points out a tangle of wires at one spot along the lines. This, he suggests, was the point from which a model UFO was suspended. Most UFO books, he says, crop the telephone lines out of the picture.

But additional studies were conducted independently by physicist Bruce Maccabbee, by researchers for Ground Saucer Watch, and by others. These studies, using computers, electron microscopes, and other equipment, concluded that the saucer was indeed a large, disk-shaped object at considerable distance and not a model suspended from the lines.

While the debate over the Trent photos was just

beginning, strange events occurred in the nighttime skies over Lubbock, Texas, in August of 1951. On the evening of August 25, four Texas Technical College professors watching for meteors saw a formation of fifteen to twenty soft, faint lights flying overhead, north to south. About an hour later, another group passed over, this time in a semicircle formation. Just before midnight, a third group appeared. The story soon made the news.

The Lubbock lights

Near midnight on August 31, an eighteen-year-old college freshman and amateur photographer, Carl Hart Jr., was lying in bed, looking through an open window. Suddenly, he saw a formation of bright lights moving across the sky. He dashed outside with his Kodak 35mm camera and took photographs of two additional formations. The photographs were printed in newspapers throughout the country and what they recorded became known as "The Lubbock Lights."

Over the next few months, the professors saw the lights twelve more times. Later, some scientists attributed the sightings to geese flying overhead, reflecting the city lights. This explanation was accepted by the Air Force. The explanation did not, however, account for the bright objects in the photographs, which were much too sharp to be flying geese.

Project Bluebook

With sightings steadily increasing, the Air Force decided in early 1952 to reorganize its own program. Project Grudge was disbanded, and Capt. Edward J. Ruppelt was placed in charge of the new program, Project Bluebook. It was Ruppelt's aim, in the next several years during which he would head the project, to keep an open mind about UFOs, as

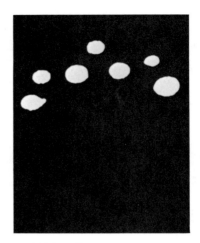

In 1951, college student Carl Hart Jr. shot this picture of a group of bright lights. Because the lights appeared in the sky over Lubbock, Texas, they became known throughout the country as "The Lubbock Lights."

The staff of Project Bluebook poses behind their seated chief, Hector Quintanilla. Project Bluebook was organized in 1952 to investigate UFOs.

much as he could within the limits placed on him. The new project was hardly underway when a sensational new series of sightings swamped the program.

The airport saucer scare

On the evening of July 19, 1952, unidentified objects appeared on radar screens at Washington National Airport. One controller, Harry G. Barnes, said, "The 'things' . . . were seven pips clustered together irregularly in one corner. . . .We knew immediately that a very strange situation existed . . . their movements were completely radical compared to those of ordinary aircraft."

Meanwhile, radar operators at nearby Andrews Air Force Base also detected the unusual objects. At the same time, various airline pilots reported "bright lights" in the skies over Washington, D.C., coinciding with the radar blips. Witnesses on the ground also saw the lights.

Finally, nearly three hours after the first contacts, Air Force jets were sent out to challenge the UFOs. Surprisingly, the objects vanished when the jets approached. The jets returned to base, and the mysterious blips, as if playing a game, reappeared on radar screens. The sightings and radar contacts continued in this manner throughout the night.

By morning, word of the sightings had leaked out. Newspapers screamed such headlines as "Jets Lose Race With Glowing Globs," "The Day the Saucers Invaded Washington, D.C.," and "Jet Flyers Told to Shoot Down Saucers." A shocked nation reeled at the very thought of flying saucers buzzing around the nation's capital.

However, the incredible story was not over yet. A week later, on the night of July 26, UFOs again appeared on radar screens. Once more, they disappeared when jets tried to intercept them. But one

On July 19, 1952, mysterious lights plagued pilots and air-traffic controllers at Washington National Airport. The darting lights amidst the planes might have looked something like this.

pilot, Lt. William Patterson, successfully spotted a cluster of "blue-white lights." As he approached the UFOs, they formed a ring around Patterson's aircraft. Frightened, Patterson radioed for instructions on what to do. In the control tower, the pilot's request was met with stunned silence. Abruptly, the UFOs broke off from the aircraft and flew away, bringing sighs of relief to pilot and control tower personnel alike.

News media demanded an explanation for the Washington National sightings. On July 29, Air Force major general John Samford, chief of Air Force Intelligence, called a press conference. He told a jam-packed audience, "The radar and visual sightings . . . were due to mirage effects created by a double-temperature inversion."

Temperature inversions occur when hot air rises higher than usual into the atmosphere. At higher altitudes, the air is normally very cold. But when the temperature pattern reverses, or "inverts," and the warm air rises, strange things can happen. Light shining through the inversion area can become distorted, especially if there are several layers of alternating hot and cold air. And radio waves can be reflected off the inversion, causing blips to appear on radar screens.

Not everyone believed this explanation for the Washington National UFOs. One United Press International reporter, writing about the incident years later, noted, "There are persons intimately involved in the July episode . . . who regard the temperature inversion explanation as no explanation." And the late University of Arizona meteorologist, Dr. James D. McDonald, observed, "When I plotted the weather data for July 19, it became quite clear that no anomalous propagation [mirage effect] could have produced the solid radar returns." Finally, the senior air traffic controller who was

In 1971, upper atmospheric testing in Florida created these colorful clouds that were mistaken for UFOs by local residents.

there through it all, Harry G. Barnes, later said, "I took the position at the time that there was something out there. My colleagues and I were convinced that something was giving us a return."

Even Project Bluebook's Captain Ruppelt was unsure of the Air Force's explanation. He classified the sightings as "unknown." He later observed, "Besides being the most highly publicized UFO sightings in the Air Force annals, they were also the most monumentally fouled-up messes that . . . [remain] in the files."

Meanwhile, certain government officials became alarmed about the public hysteria over flying saucers. A secret meeting was ordered. The course they were about to take would affect U.S. UFO policy for decades to come.

3

Coverups and Conspiracies: Searching for Answers

IN THE WAKE of the Washington National scare and mounting public concern, government officials felt pressured to act. On January 14, 1953, the Central Intelligence Agency (CIA) held a secret four-day meeting. At that meeting, scientists and Air Force officials discussed what to do about the UFO "problem."

This group was commissioned by the White House to find out if UFOs posed a threat to national security. It was also asked to recommend a course of action. The group became known as the Robertson Panel, named after its chairman, physicist H.P. Robertson.

Military officials briefed panel members on current UFO policy. They also discussed some of the important cases on file, and reviewed the general evidence.

On January 18, the panel concluded that UFOs posed no threat to U.S. security. Members did ex-

On July 16, 1952, Coast Guard photographer Shell Alpert grabbed his camera and photographed these mysterious lights as they appeared over Salem, Massachusetts.

41

press concern, however, that unfriendly nations could use "false" UFO sightings as a "cover" during an attack. This would cause military phone lines to be jammed with calls from frightened citizens, at a time when communication would be most important.

This reasoning was enough for the panelists. In their final report, they recommended "that the national security agencies take immediate steps to strip the Unidentified Flying Objects of the special status" and "aura of mystery they have unfortunately acquired." They said, too, that these agencies should find ways to convince the public that UFOs were not real.

The panel also recommended that Project Bluebook be continued at its current level. However, it suggested that the emphasis be placed on an "educational program of training and debunking." With UFOs thus "explained away," the panel felt that the threat of clogged telephone lines would be greatly reduced.

Panel did not consider the evidence well

One person in attendance was uncomfortable with the panel's recommendations. Dr. J. Allen Hynek, Project Bluebook's scientific consultant, felt the panel could not make a sound decision on UFOs after only four days. And a disturbing thought was slowly brewing in Hynek's mind. What if there were, after all, much more to the UFO mystery than the mere misidentifications he was hired to detect?

The "debunking" policy was now in full effect. Air Force officials believed UFOs would soon be "explained away" and forgotten by the public. These hopes were quickly demolished, however, with the 1953 publication of Donald Keyhoe's second best-seller, *Flying Saucers from Outer Space*. In this book, the author further accused the Air Force

Dr. J. Allen Hynek (left) consults Police Chief Robert R. Taylor of Dexter, Michigan, as the two men investigate a rash of UFO sightings in southern Michigan.

of withholding information. To him, the military's debunking efforts were proof enough of a grand plot, a deliberate attempt to cover up the facts.

Keyhoe was now firmly convinced that UFOs were spacecraft from other worlds. He strongly recommended that Project Bluebook be expanded and that plans be made for face-to-face contact with the space aliens.

When people read Keyhoe's book, they were not ready to believe the Air Force's explanations or forget about UFOs. And further sensational sightings seemed to confirm Keyhoe's opinions that UFOs were indeed from outer space.

UFOs over English air bases

On the night of August 13, 1956, an event occurred that baffled investigators and the public alike. Ground observers spotted a mysterious "luminous object" in the skies. Radar controllers locked onto the object as it traveled the distance between the Bentwaters and Lakenheath air bases in eastern England.

A jet was sent to intercept the UFO. During pursuit, the object was simultaneously tracked from the ground, from the air, and by visual sighting. At one point the object abruptly vanished from the pursuing jet's radar screen and appeared about fifteen seconds later *behind* the jet. The pilot tried unsuccessfully to shake the trailing UFO. After another ten minutes, the object became stationary, and the jet returned to base. After a second jet gave up pursuit due to engine troubles, the object moved out of range of radar screens.

Years later, the University of Colorado's Condon Report labeled this sighting "the most puzzling and

UFO sightings have occurred throughout the world.

UFO SIGHTINGS

Arctic Ocean

GREENLAND

NORTH AMERICA

Atlantic Ocean

Pacific Ocean

SOUTH AMERICA

unusual case in the radar-visual files. . . . The apparently rational, intelligent behavior of the UFO suggests a mechanical device of unknown origin as the most probable explanation of this sighting."

Despite the baffling nature of the case, Project Bluebook continued its policy of "explaining away." At this point, Donald Keyhoe became fed up with the Air Force. In October of 1956, he formed his own UFO research organization, the National Investigations Committee on Aerial Phenomena

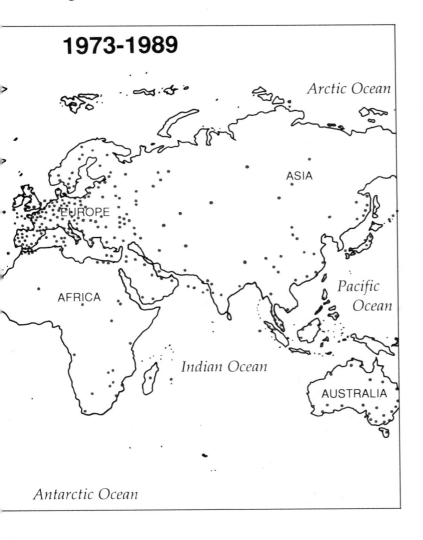

When it reappeared from behind the peak, it was lower, larger, and flying in the opposite direction, so fast that the next two shots were lost.

A UFO hovers over a peak before zooming off.

(NICAP). Keyhoe established tough membership standards. He accepted mostly applicants with academic degrees or knowledge in various scientific fields.

Keyhoe had various goals for NICAP. He wanted to collect and document the best sightings and to convince the public that flying saucers were from outer space. He also planned to lobby Congress for hearings and force the Air Force to "tell the truth."

In the meantime, an important new book appeared, offering an insider's look at Project Bluebook: *The Report on Unidentified Flying Objects,* by former Bluebook director Captain Ruppelt. In it, Ruppelt, who had left Bluebook in September of 1953, criticized Keyhoe for his methods. He did, however, show a surprisingly open attitude about UFOs. In the book's final sentence, Ruppelt even said that maybe some UFOs would prove to be "interplanetary spaceships."

More controversial photos

Then, in January of 1958, another sensational story appeared in the press, together with an amazing set of photographs. As the story goes, professional photographer Almiro Barauna was aboard a Brazilian navy ship, off the coast of Trindade Island. From the ship, he saw a Saturn-shaped object hovering over the island. He took a series of four photographs and developed them on board. Later, he submitted them to military officials. The officials promptly declared the photographs genuine. The photos were then released to the press by the president of Brazil.

Eventually, a scientist found out that Barauna was a trick photographer. He also discovered that Barauna had once published a humorous article, along with admittedly fake UFO photos. Because of this, some researchers thought the Trindade photos were also fakes. And others doubted Barauna's story because no one else on the ship saw the UFO.

Members of Ground Saucer Watch, a U.S. UFO research organization, decided to study the photos. They used computers and other equipment to improve the quality of the pictures. After much study, they concluded that the photographs were real.

With the Barauna case and others like it, the public did not know what to think. On one side were the military and government agencies, declaring that UFOs did not exist. On the other side were the UFO groups and Keyhoe, declaring that spaceships from other worlds were visiting the earth.

Another controversy

As the 1950s came to a close, a new controversy took place. It further convinced ufologists that there was an ongoing conspiracy to conceal the truth about UFOs. In 1959 a new printing of Ruppelt's *Report on Unidentified Flying Objects* came on the market. This version contained an important difference from the original. Ruppelt had added three new chapters. In contrast to the balanced nature of the original seventeen chapters, the three new chapters were completely negative. Furthermore, there was nothing in the book to indicate revision. The original 1956 copyright appeared just as it had in the earlier edition, with no reference to changes.

No one has ever explained why the changes were made. But ufologists believed that the changes were forced on Ruppelt, perhaps by military or government officials unhappy with the book. To the ufologists, it was just one more example of the government trying to hide the truth about UFOs.

4

Contact with Humanoids: Three Cases That Shocked the World

DONALD KEYHOE'S NICAP organization was very skillful at gathering UFO reports. It was equally skillful at accusing the military of cover-ups and conspiracies. But it was weak in collecting reports involving contacts with "humanoids" or other creatures associated with UFOs.

Humanoids, or humanlike creatures, are the most common type of beings reported. They usually appear to be about three or four feet tall, with slender bodies, bald heads, and slanted eyes. A second common type of being is also human in appearance, except that it is usually dressed in a uniform. A third, less common type is the short "hairy dwarf."

NICAP's policy of ignoring contact reports was undoubtedly due to the ridicule associated with the contactees. Contactees were people who claimed they had personal and repeated contact with wise, mystical "space brothers."

The contactees told colorful stories of rides to

An artist's picture of an alien is based on witnesses' descriptions of the mysterious creature.

49

other planets aboard flying saucers. They also gave their followers special messages, which they claimed to have received from the space brothers. These messages usually warned of the dangers of war and offered hope of a better world to come. There was nothing in the messages, however, to show that the contacts really took place.

So much ridicule was heaped upon the contactees by scientists that Keyhoe and other serious UFO researchers avoided any kind of association with the contactees. As a result, NICAP refused to accept *any* kinds of contact reports.

Eventually, however, a turn of events forced NICAP and other groups to pay attention. Increasing numbers of reports, filed by scared and confused witnesses, told of sightings of strange creatures from UFOs. In these cases, there were no rides to other worlds, repeated contacts, or messages for humanity. There were only frightened witnesses who wanted explanations for their experiences.

Over the years, witnesses have reported many such contacts. There are three particular cases, however, that strongly influenced the direction of UFO research.

On June 26 and 27, 1959, Father William B. Gill of Boianai, Papua New Guinea claimed to have seen waving aliens perched on top of a space ship.

The visitation in New Guinea

The first case occurred on two consecutive evenings, June 26 and 27, 1959, near the Anglican mission of Father William B. Gill, in Boianai, Papua New Guinea. Most of the incidents were witnessed not only by Father Gill but also by about twenty-five natives (most of them children), teachers, and medical technicians. Many times the witnesses saw a bright, sparkling UFO, sometimes with humanoid figures standing on top.

One time Father Gill and some of the natives waved at the humanoids and watched as they waved

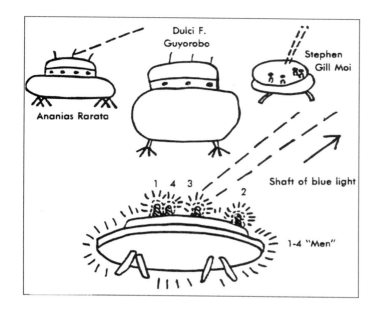

Dulci F. Guyorobo

Stephen Gill Moi

Ananias Rarata

1 4 3 2

Shaft of blue light

1-4 "Men"

Witnesses' drawings of the UFO sighting in Boianai, Papua New Guinea.

back. They also watched the UFO aim a blue beam of light upward from the craft.

The late Harvard astronomer and UFO skeptic Dr. Donald H. Menzel came up with an explanation. He said that Gill might be a victim of myopia, or nearsightedness. In other words, he could see close objects clearly, but objects at a distance would appear blurred. According to Menzel, what Gill saw as humanoids aboard a UFO was merely a blurred view of his own eyelashes and the planet Venus!

A priest would not lie

Investigators found that Gill was indeed nearsighted. But they also determined that he was wearing glasses during the sightings. Ufologists dismissed Menzel's explanation. Gill, they pointed out, had recognized the planet Venus as a separate object in his earliest reports. To them, Gill's status as a priest—a man not likely to lie—gave considerable weight to the case.

The second important contact case is one of the most sensational and thoroughly studied cases in

UFO history. It occurred on the night of September 19, 1961. Barney and Betty Hill were driving along U.S. Route 3 near Groveton, New Hampshire, when they spotted a glowing UFO in the sky. They stopped their car, and Barney got out. As the UFO approached, Barney watched through binoculars. He saw humanoid figures in the windows of the UFO. Frightened, he jumped back into the car and sped off.

As the Hills raced away, they heard mysterious beeping sounds and experienced drowsy, tingling sensations. Then they heard the beeping sounds again. They suddenly realized that they were now thirty-five miles farther down the road, with no idea

Mr. and Mrs. Barney Hill hold a copy of the book that details their encounter with a UFO.

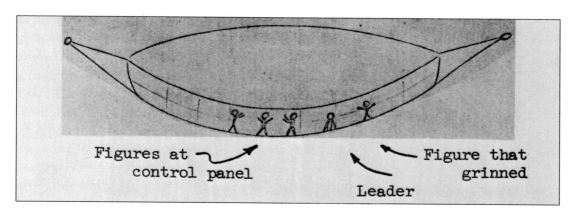

Figures at control panel

Figure that grinned

Leader

of how they got there. They noticed that their watches had stopped. Too tired to think much more of it, they drove home.

Later, under questioning by UFO investigators, the Hills realized that they had arrived home from the trip two hours later than they should have. They could not account for the missing two hours.

Hills suffer psychological trauma

The Hills began to suffer emotional problems because of their experiences. Betty, in particular, had recurring dreams about being taken aboard a UFO and undergoing medical examinations. Eventually, the couple sought treatment from Dr. Benjamin Simon, a highly respected Boston psychiatrist. Dr. Simon decided to put the couple under regressive hypnosis, a technique used by mental health professionals to help patients "relive" forgotten memories. It helps the mind recall memories of things that actually happened or things that the mind *thinks* has happened.

Over a period of time, under separate, tape-recorded regressive hypnosis sessions, the Hills indeed relived their experiences. Their story, as told to Simon, follows.

After the first series of beeps, Barney and Betty Hill were taken aboard the UFO by slender, uni-

Sketch by Barney Hill showing aliens in an airship.

While under hypnosis, Barney Hill gave this description of the creature that abducted him.

formed humanoids. These beings had large slanted eyes, bald heads, no noses, and slitlike mouths. Barney and Betty were taken into separate rooms and given medical examinations. The humanoids examined Barney's mouth, checked his back, and placed a large, circular device around his groin area. They examined Betty's skin, scraped skin samples from her arm, and inserted a long needle into her navel, supposedly to do a pregnancy test. The creatures "spoke" to the Hills by projecting thoughts into their minds.

Betty asked the humanoids where they came from. One of them showed her a star map, with lines drawn between the stars. The lines, she was told, represented trade routes between star systems. (During one of the hypnosis sessions, Betty drew a picture of this map.)

Then, the couple was released, and the Hills found themselves thirty-five miles down the road. Their conscious memories of the incident had been wiped out.

This shocking account of abduction, or kidnapping, by creatures from a UFO was widely covered in magazine articles. It was also reported in detail in John G. Fuller's best-selling book, *The Interrupted Journey.* Later, it was also portrayed for millions of viewers in a 1975 TV movie, *The UFO Incident.*

Hills experience Betty's fantasy?

Many ufologists were convinced that the Hill case represented the best evidence yet of possible extraterrestrial visitation. It was Simon's opinion, however, that the abduction part of the story was fantasy. He thought it had grown out of Betty's constant retelling of her dreams.

In 1969, an Ohio school teacher, Marjorie Fish, wondered if the star map patterns reported by Betty might help prove that the incident was real. Fish interviewed Betty (Barney had died of a stroke earlier that year) and studied a number of star catalogs. From the catalogs, she constructed some three-dimensional models. For this, she used beads hanging from strings to represent stars.

Fish limited her selection to the stars within fifty-five light-years of earth. She then viewed the models from different angles, searching for patterns to match the Hill map. It was not until a new star catalog was published, however, and a new model constructed, that she found a matching pattern. From this, she concluded that the home base of the humanoids was the double star system Zeta Reticuli. The match seemed to strengthen the Hills' story.

Since then, scientists studying the case have found similar patterns with other star systems, which means the Zeta Reticuli system is not the only possible origin of the UFO. Heated debate continues to rage between ufologists and scientists about this most perplexing case.

The Socorro landing case

The third important contact case took place at about 5:45 P.M. on April 24, 1964. Police officer Lonnie Zamora was chasing a speeding automobile outside of Socorro, New Mexico. He heard a loud roar and saw a blue-orange flame streaking downward from the sky. He immediately gave up pursuit of the speeder and followed a steep, rough road toward the apparent landing site. Zamora then spotted a shiny, metallic object down in a shallow gully, about eight hundred feet away.

"It was egg-shaped with one end, which I figure was the front, sort of tapered," said Zamora. "It was white and smooth, with no windows or openings of any kind. It was sitting on legs about four feet tall and seemed to be about the size of a car." Zamora saw two figures outside the object. "I couldn't see

Artist's depiction of police officer Lonnie Zamoro as he appeared on April 24, 1964, when he spotted a UFO in Socorro, New Mexico.

any features," he said, "just two figures in the distance. . . . They looked about four feet high."

The police officer then drove farther down the road, stopped about one hundred feet from the object and got out of his car. The figures were no longer there. As he stepped toward the object, Zamora noticed a red insignia, about two feet in height, on the front of the craft. "There were markings in red letters about a foot high on the side. It looked like a crescent with a vertical arrow pointed upward inside the crescent and a horizontal bar beneath that."

At first there was a thunderous roar. Fearing that the object might explode, Zamora fled. At about two hundred feet away, he turned around to see the object rising upward. Zamora said, "There was no noise. It was about two hundred feet off the ground just hovering." Then, several seconds later, the object took off rapidly to the southwest. As Zamora radioed for help, he noticed that several mesquite bushes around the landing area were burning.

Soon after, Sgt. Sam Chavez of the state police force joined Zamora in an examination of the site. In addition to some burnt bushes, they found four impressions in the ground. Chavez took photographs of the area.

The impressions, squarish in shape, formed an irregular pattern in the ground. Three of the four burnt spots were within the area of the impressions. Several other smaller impressions were later labeled as "footprints" by the Air Force. Soil samples were taken from the site to various laboratories for analysis. Test results, however, revealed no materials new to science.

J. Allen Hynek, called in to investigate the incident for the Air Force, hailed the case as one of the best on record. He declared that he was "more puzzled than when I arrived." Project Bluebook listed the case as "unidentified." Even NICAP was impressed, breaking from its previous "no contact cases" policy to investigate the report.

Equally important, Zamora's standing as an honest and reliable police officer gave many people reason to believe that a spaceship had landed at Socorro, New Mexico. Newspapers and magazines covered the story nationwide. NICAP called for congressional investigations.

Obviously, cases of this nature could no longer be ignored. The pressure was mounting to do something about UFOs.

5

From Swamp Gas to Congressional Hearings: Dawn of the UFO Era

WHEN THE ZAMORA case hit the headlines in April 1964, NICAP was ready. The organization sent to every member of Congress a copy of its 184-page report, *The UFO Evidence*. The report cited 746 sightings. Included were observations and testimony from Army, Navy, Marine, and Air Force personnel as well as statements from pilots, scientists, engineers, police officers, and other professionals.

The report also presented cases involving stalled automobiles, television interference, radar contacts, unusual sounds, and physical effects, all reportedly caused by UFOs. Additionally, the report criticized the Air Force's handling of UFO reports. It then called for a "scientific and political review of the entire UFO situation."

Release of the report symbolized a gradual change in the public's perception of unidentified aerial phenomena. In the 1950s, people firmly viewed UFOs as flying saucers—possibly hostile

The weather bureau was unable to explain these mysterious flashes that appeared in the Kentucky sky in 1947.

spaceships from other worlds. By the mid-1960s, however, people became more conscious of the "unidentified" aspects of UFOs. They might be spaceships from other worlds, or they might be something else. But whatever their nature, they were likely to be worthy of serious study.

Reflecting this increasingly serious treatment of unexplained reports, the term *unidentified flying object* quickly replaced the term *flying saucer*. Newspapers, magazines, books, and case reports filed by investigators began to use the newer term.

Some members of Congress began paying attention to NICAP's call for UFO hearings. However, there still was not quite enough momentum to bring about the hearings. It would take a series of sensational sightings over the next few years to do that.

Incidents at Exeter

At 2:00 A.M. on the moonless night of September 3, 1965, near the small town of Exeter, New Hampshire, eighteen-year-old Norman Muscarello was hitchhiking along Route 150. He was on his way home. Suddenly, a bright, glowing object moved toward him over an open field. Frightened, Muscarello jumped into a ditch and watched as the object passed overhead and drifted toward a nearby house. He observed that it had red, pulsating lights, and he guessed that it was about eighty feet wide. He then ran to the road, where an elderly couple drove him to the Exeter police station.

Meanwhile, Exeter patrolman Eugene Bertrand came across a woman parked near a Route 101 bypass. She was upset and told Bertrand that a silent object with red, flashing lights had followed her for nine miles along the road. After this, Bertrand was summoned to the police station to hear Muscarello's story.

The officer decided to take Muscarello back to

On September 3, 1965, hitchhiker Norman Muscarello spotted a glowing object in the New Hampshire sky. Sixty other witnesses reported similar sightings.

the scene of his sighting. At first they saw nothing. Then, unexpectedly, horses in a nearby corral began kicking and whinnying. Dogs in the area began barking. Then Muscarello shouted, "I see it! I see it!"

From behind two tall pines, a bright, round object rose, wobbling slightly, bathing the entire area in a bright red light. Fearing radiation, Bertrand pulled Muscarello back toward the police car. He called the station, crying, "My God! I see the damn thing myself!"

Another police car pulled up, and Officer David Hunt stepped out just in time to see the object before it disappeared.

Investigation of the case by journalist John G. Fuller revealed there were another sixty witnesses

Exeter patrolman Eugene Bertrand sits with mouth agape as flashing lights appear in the New Hampshire sky.

who saw similar objects in the area. Most of the sightings took place over a period of several weeks in the fall, usually near power lines. Fuller's investigations resulted in another book, *Incident at Exeter*.

The Pentagon initially attributed the Muscarello sighting to military aircraft exercises (which actually occurred beforehand). Officials later admitted that the Air Force had no explanation. UFO skeptic Phillip Klass, meanwhile, suggested that the Exeter sightings were caused by ball lightning. Ball lightning is a rare form of electrical energy. Under certain conditions, it appears as a glowing ball of light, usually along power lines. Ancient sailors used to report ball lightning on ships' masts, during electrical storms. They called it St. Elmo's fire.

Officer Bertrand, however, did not agree with Klass's explanation: "I know there was some kind of flying craft. I was in the Air Force, refueling, mostly ground work, and I know aircraft make noise. This one didn't. It was silent. No hum. Nothing. Just moving through the air silently. And the light, so bright it lighted up the whole field. There was something there. Dave Hunt and the kid saw it. We weren't all seeing something that wasn't there."

The O'Brien Report

Months later, in February 1966, a committee of scientists, headed by Dr. Brian O'Brien, met for one day to discuss Bluebook's problems in explaining the Exeter UFOs and other reports. The committee supported the Air Force viewpoint but felt it was time for a change. They issued a report, later known as the O'Brien Report. In it, they recommended that the Air Force turn over the study of UFOs to a university.

If the uproar over the Exeter sightings was not enough to cause the final embarrassment to the Air

Force, some widely publicized sightings near Dexter and Hillsdale, Michigan, were. The sightings took place in March 1966, over swampy areas of land. Witnesses reported seeing strange, glowing lights in the night sky.

The Air Force was pressured to explain the sightings, so they sent J. Allen Hynek to investigate. Hynek found that the community was "gripped with near hysteria" over the sightings.

After investigating, Hynek called a news conference, with over one hundred reporters attending. He said that the sightings were probably caused by swamp gas (also known as "fox fire" or "will o' the wisp"). Swamp gas is floating, glowing gas released

In 1966, Dr. J. Allen Hynek displays an image of an apparent UFO during a news conference. Hynek concluded that the image was probably caused by floating swamp gas.

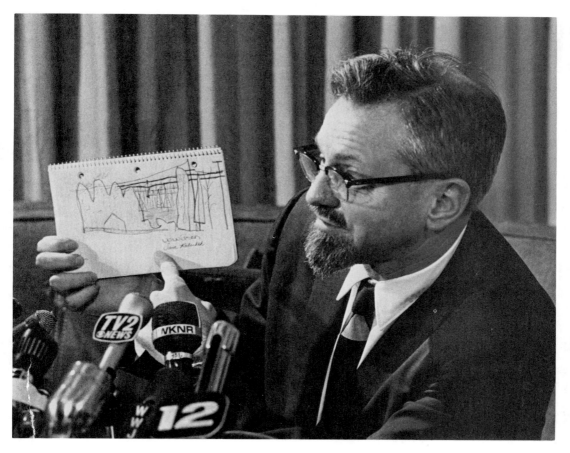

Alien talk shows

from decaying swamp plants. Hynek told reporters, "A dismal swamp is a most unlikely place for a visit from outer space."

Some of the witnesses were unhappy with the official explanation. "I think the Air Force is full of malarkey," said police sergeant Nuel Schneider. "I know what I saw. We got a call on one that went by and lit the whole city [Milan, Michigan] up. We saw about three of them way off. We got closer to Milan, in a cornfield, and started taking pictures. We watched it from 2:00 in the morning until 7:00. A top turned upside down is what it looked like to us. We saw lights and we could see something of a form when we got binoculars."

At least sixty-two students in Hillsdale watched the pulsating UFOs from their dormitory windows. One, Cynthia Poffenberger, said a UFO "went right in front of my window." Another, Barbara Kohn, said one of the UFOs "was like a squashed football."

Media maligns witnesses

The swamp gas story quickly hit the news wires, resulting in ridicule aimed at Hynek and the Air Force. The irony of this whole affair was that Hynek had by now personally changed his stance on UFOs. The Zamora case had convinced him that UFOs represented something very real. He believed, however, that the Michigan sightings really were examples of swamp gas.

The clamor over the sightings was so great that two Michigan congressmen, Weston E. Vivian and Gerald R. Ford, called for congressional hearings. Ford, later to become president of the United States, said, "The American public deserves a better explanation than that thus far given by the Air Force."

On April 5, 1966, the House Armed Services

Committee conducted open hearings on the UFO situation. Only three people testified. They were Secretary of the Air Force Harold D. Brown, current Project Bluebook chief Hector Quintanilla, and J. Allen Hynek. After Secretary Brown outlined the Air Force view, Hynek spoke, saying that UFOs deserved serious scientific attention. The Air Force assumption that all UFOs had conventional explanations, he warned, "may turn out to be a roadblock in the pursuit of research endeavors." He then recommended that the study of UFOs be turned over to a civilian panel of scientists.

When the hearings concluded, Secretary Brown acted on the recommendations of Hynek and the O'Brien Report. He ordered the Air Force chief of staff to contract with scientists and a leading university to study UFOs. In essence, the Air Force was admitting that its own study was inadequate.

Baffling mutilations

Meanwhile, some strange events were going on in farmland areas across the United States. Farmers were finding the mutilated bodies of cows and horses on their lands. The animals were usually found with vital organs removed and blood drained. Sometimes external parts such as skin, eyes, and head were surgically removed.

At the same time, officials received reports of strange, unidentified lights in the sky. The appearance of the lights and the absence of footprints around the animal remains led some people to link the two. They thought that UFOs were picking up the animals and doing the mutilations while hovering overhead. They would then drop the remains to the ground.

The best-known mutilation case is that of Snippy, an Appaloosa pony whose body was found on September 15, 1967, after being missing for several

This Appaloosa pony was found dead and mutilated on September 15, 1967. Some researchers maintain that UFOs were the culprit.

days. He was skinned, with bleached bones showing around the skull and shoulders. Vital organs were missing, but there was no blood in the body or on the ground. Snippy's tracks ended about one hundred feet away from where his body was found, and there were no footprints in that area. A recent, local rash of UFO sightings convinced some investigators that UFOs were involved.

Most UFO investigators later concluded that cults were responsible for this and other mutilation cases. The cultists, they said, used the removed blood and organs in mysterious satanic rites. There are still some researchers, however, who believe UFOs were responsible.

Scientific study ordered

In the meantime, the Air Force moved to rid itself of UFO study. On October 7, 1967, officials announced that the University of Colorado, in Boulder, would conduct an impartial scientific study of UFOs. The study would be under the direction of physicist Dr. Edward U. Condon. The results eventually became known as the Condon Report.

Over the next few years, as problems and controversies over the Condon Report developed, rumors began to circulate that the study would decide that UFOs were not worthy of further scientific study. Again, those chosen to study the UFOs believed they were of natural or human-made origin. They wanted to conclude the study as soon as possible. NICAP and other groups, initially led to believe the study would be impartial, were furious. The pressure on Congress to conduct additional hearings, continued.

Full congressional hearings

Finally, Congress relented. On July 29, 1968, the House Committee on Science and Astronautics held a full-fledged, scientific hearing on UFOs. Six scientists, including J. Allen Hynek, James E. McDonald, Carl Sagan, and James A. Harder, spoke at the hearings. Six more scientists sent papers, including Donald M. Menzel, R. Leo Sprinkle, and Stanton T. Friedman.

Hynek testified, "I do not feel that I can be labeled a flying saucer 'believer'—my swamp gas record in the Michigan melee should suffice to squash any such ideas—but I do feel that even though this may be an area of scientific quicksand, signals continue to point to a mystery that needs to be solved. . . . I feel that there exists a phenomenon eminently worthy of study. . . . We want to find out what it's all about."

McDonald, from the University of Arizona, was even more blunt. He said, "My position is that UFOs are entirely real and we do not know what they are, because we have laughed them out of court. The possibility that these are extraterrestrial devices, that we are dealing with surveillance from some advanced technology, is a possibility I take

Noted physicist Dr. Edward U. Condon headed a scientific study of UFOs. Known as the Condon Report, the results indicated that UFOs could be explained by natural or human-made phenomena.

very seriously."

And nuclear physicist Stanton T. Friedman was even more convinced that UFOs were real. In his submitted paper, he wrote, "I have concluded that the earth is being visited by intelligently controlled vehicles whose origin is extraterrestrial."

Not all the scientists agreed that UFOs were extraterrestrial craft. Carl Sagan, a strong supporter of the radio signal search for extraterrestrial life, said, "I would of course demand very firm evidence before I would say [the extraterrestrial explanation] seems to be a very likely hypothesis. . . . If Congress is interested in a pursuit of the question of extraterrestrial life, I believe it would be much better advised to support . . . the radio astronomy programs of the National Science Foundation, than to pour very much money into this study of UFOs."

Menzel, who liked to call himself "the man who killed Santa Claus," submitted his opinion in writ-

Scientist Carl Sagan stands in front of a radio telescope that uses radio signals to search for signs of extraterrestrial life.

ing. He wrote that "natural explanations exist for the unexplained sightings. . . . The question of UFOs has become one of faith and belief, rather than one of science. . . . Reopening the subject of UFOs makes just about as much sense as reopening the subject of witchcraft."

The hearings were important because as a whole, they represented the first scientific testimony in favor of UFOs. Before the hearings, few scientists would even admit an interest in the subject. Afterward, the opportunity was there for other scientists to "come out of the closet" and speak openly.

But ominous storm clouds rumbled on the horizon. The Condon Report was about to be released. What it had to say about UFOs would not make Donald Keyhoe, NICAP, and other UFO believers very happy.

6

The Condon Report: An Attempt to Write Off UFOs

W HEN THE AIR FORCE announced in October 1967 that it was funding the University of Colorado to do a scientific study of UFOs, hopes were high among UFO researchers that the project would conduct an impartial investigation. Many UFO investigators, including long-time antagonist Donald E. Keyhoe, applauded the Air Force's decision. Some even volunteered to help.

Long before the announcement, however, the seeds of trouble were planted. Arguments developed over staff makeup, research methods, and project goals. The scientist named to head the study, Dr. Edward U. Condon, revealed his attitude by making public fun of UFOs. And in August 1966, project administrator Robert J. Low made the following comments in a memo to another planner:

In October 1981, Hanna McRoberts unknowingly captured this image of a UFO when she photographed a hill on Vancouver Island in Canada.

The trick would be, I think, to describe the project so that, to the public, it would appear a totally objective study, but, to the scientific community, would present

71

Robert J. Low, administrator of a scientific UFO study, shared Edward Condon's skeptical view that UFO sightings were imaginary.

the image of a group of nonbelievers trying their best to be objective, but having almost zero expectation of finding a saucer. One way to do this would be to stress investigation, not of the physical phenomena, but rather the people who do the observing—the psychology and sociology of the persons and groups who report seeing UFOs.

In other words, Low wanted the public to think the project was doing a thorough, balanced study of UFOs. At the same time, he wanted other scientists to know that the group was skeptical. He suggested that the study concentrate on the people who reported UFOs. He believed that UFO sightings were imaginary—that people were either seeing things or they were mentally imbalanced. The study would not, apparently, do much to study the UFOs themselves. Low's memo, then, seemed to suggest that the project was stacked against UFOs from the start.

As the project took form, one staff member, Dr. David R. Saunders, became upset at the direction the project was taking. He soon came into conflict with Low and others who supported Condon's views.

Low's memo was discovered in July 1967 by staff member Roy Craig. Eventually, the memo went through Saunders and Keyhoe and on to Dr. James E. McDonald. Condon was furious about the leak. He accused Saunders of stealing the memo from Low's files and fired him.

Flying saucer fiasco

The story broke to the public in May 1968, with the publication of John G. Fuller's *Look* magazine article, entitled "Flying Saucer Fiasco." Keyhoe then announced that NICAP had withdrawn its support of the project. Congressman J. Edward Roush, expressing "grave doubts as to the . . . objectivity of the project," called for new congressional hearings, to be held two months later.

Meanwhile, work on the project continued. Team

members conducted field investigations, wrote reports, and analyzed the personalities of those reporting UFOs.

In November 1968, and prior to any public announcements, Condon turned over the final report to the National Academy of Sciences for review. The Academy rubber-stamped its approval. It declared that the study made a "creditable effort" in using science to solve the UFO problem.

Then, in March 1969, the Condon committee released its final report. It was issued to the public in a 967-page book titled *Scientific Study of Unidentified Flying Objects*. Proponents of serious UFO study cringed as they read the conclusions. The report said that "UFO phenomena do not offer a fruitful field in which to look for major scientific discoveries." It also said that:

• "We do not think that at this time the federal government ought to set up a major new agency . . . for the scientific study of UFOs."

• "We have no evidence of secrecy concerning UFO reports."

• "The subject of UFOs has been widely misrepresented to the public by a small number of individuals."

• "We found that no direct evidence whatsoever of a convincing nature now exists for the claim that any UFOs represent spacecraft visiting Earth from another civilization."

Reporters treat evidence casually

Most reporters saw nothing but the conclusions and recommendations of the report. These were written by Condon himself and passed out to the press. Few bothered to examine the full report.

Astonishingly, the full report contains some comments that are in direct conflict with Condon's conclusions. If reporters and other scientists had only

An illustration entered into the Congressional Record depicts commonly described UFO shapes.

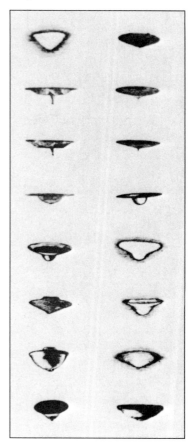

read these comments, they might have questioned the conclusions. Buried deep in the contents of the report were statements such as the following:

• "An extraordinary flying object, silvery, metallic, disk-shaped . . . and evidently artificial, flew within sight of the two witnesses." (The Paul Trent/ McMinnville case.)

• "Analysis indicates that the images of the film are difficult to reconcile with aircraft or other known phenomena."

• "The probability that at least one genuine UFO was involved appears to be fairly high."

• "This must remain as one of the most puzzling radar cases on record, and no conclusion is possible at this time."

• "It does appear that this defies explanation by conventional means."

• "The three unexplained sightings which have been gleaned from a great mass of reports are a challenge to the analyst."

Furthermore, 30 percent of the cases studied by the Condon team were unexplained. Even the Air Force did not have such a high rate of unexplained cases.

Condon's conclusions are believed

If nothing else, these comments and statistics should have stirred further scientific interest. But because few people examined the details, Condon's conclusions received all the attention. Coming from a seemingly authoritative source, they served to settle the issue in the minds of many scientists, journalists, and politicians.

One Condon Report staff member, however, openly disagreed with the findings. David R. Saunders, who was fired earlier, teamed with journalist R. Roger Harkins to write the book *UFOs? Yes! Where the Condon Committee Went Wrong.* It

"STAY CALM, DR. CONDON—JUST TELL THEM YOU
DON'T BELIEVE IN THEM!"

was published just after the Condon Report was released. Saunders charged that the project was biased
against UFOs from the very start. He also said that
its research methods were poor. He questioned how
the study could deny the existence of UFOs when
30 percent of the cases studied were unexplained.

Hynek also criticized the report. He said that it
was wrong to include so many weak and explainable cases in the study. He also said it was wrong to
staff the project with inexperienced people who
knew little about UFOs. He scolded the project for
attempting to dismiss a phenomenon that "cannot be
readily waved away."

Scientists support report

Many scientists, however, supported the report.
Astronomer Dr. Donald E. Ehlers said that the
Condon Committee was to be commended for dis-
counting "a growing religion." And biologist Dr.

Hudson Hoagland said that the study added "massive additional weight to the already overwhelming improbability of visits by UFOs guided by intelligent beings."

The Condon Report had a devastating effect on the field of UFO study. A major consequence was the closure of Project Bluebook. On December 17, 1969, Air Force Secretary Robert C. Seamans announced that the project could not "be justified either on the grounds of national security or in the interest of science."

UFO groups decline in membership

Another effect was a decrease in membership in NICAP and other UFO groups. These were now the only organizations handling UFO reports. As NICAP struggled, however, a new, smaller group was forming, called MUFON, the Midwest UFO

Speakers at a Mutual UFO Network (MUFON) conference debate the existence of UFOs.

Network. Later this organization would become the Mutual UFO Network. It would grow to become the largest UFO organization in the United States.

A circular indentation in a beanfield in Iowa appears to be the landing site of a UFO that was spotted on July 13, 1969.

The Barr beanfield case

Though interest in UFOs dropped sharply after the Condon Report was released, sightings continued to occur. One of the most famous was the Barr beanfield case. The incident took place on a farm near Garrison, Iowa, on the night of July 13, 1969. On that date, two teenagers, Patti Barr and her cousin Kathy Mahr, heard a loud, roaring sound. They looked through an upstairs bedroom window to see a large, rotating, orange, glowing, oval-shaped object. It had a double row of lights across its middle and was hovering over an adjoining soybean field.

After a few moments, the object suddenly "winked out" and took off at high speed. The spot in the beanfield where the UFO hovered only moments before now glowed red.

The next morning, the girls told Patti's father about the sighting. At first he was skeptical. He declared the incident to be "a figment of their imagination." Later, however, he found a large circular patch in the beanfield, in the area where the girls saw the UFO. Plants inside the forty-foot-diameter patch were wilted, as if blasted by intense heat.

Though some local residents attribute the case to lightning, most UFO investigators consider the case unsolved. Patti herself said that it was an "air-flying object from outer space," something that "wasn't anything earthly."

The Delphos, Kansas, landing

An even more famous case is the Delphos, Kansas, "landing." On the evening of November 2, 1971, sixteen-year old Ronald Johnson heard a rumbling sound while outside. He saw a brightly lit object about seventy-five feet away, hovering several feet above the ground. He ran for his parents and returned to see the UFO take off in the southern sky.

Later, Ronald's parents found a glowing, ring-shaped area at the landing spot. They touched the

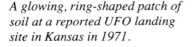

A glowing, ring-shaped patch of soil at a reported UFO landing site in Kansas in 1971.

ring soil (consisting of a mysterious white material) and noticed that the ends of their fingers became numb. A later investigation of the site also revealed an overhanging limb with heat blisters. The investigators also verified that the soil in the ring area was different from the surrounding soil. All of these things seemed to indicate that the boy's story was true.

Soil analysis, however, revealed that a fungus growth could have been responsible for the ring shape and soil changes. Left unexplained, however, were the glowing effects, the numb feelings, and the heat blisters on the plants.

Second thoughts about UFOs

During 1972, interest in UFOs was still low. Before the year was over, however, two books appeared that reflected a subtle but serious backlash to the Condon Report. These books encouraged some scientists to have second thoughts about UFOs.

One book was *UFOs—A Scientific Debate,* edited by Carl Sagan and Thornton Page. It presented a variety of pro and con scientific papers. In presenting both sides of the issue, it was more fair to the subject than the Condon Report.

The other was the long-awaited book by Dr. J. Allen Hynek, *The UFO Experience: A Scientific Inquiry.* In this one book, Hynek was considered to have offered the most thoughtful and sensible arguments ever made for the continued scientific study of UFOs. Hynek had by now come full circle and emerged as the most prominent spokesman in the field. Hynek not only recommended further studies but presented a system for rating the quality of UFO reports. He clarified many misconceptions about UFOs and criticized the methods and conclusions of the Condon Report.

Most important of all, Hynek introduced a new

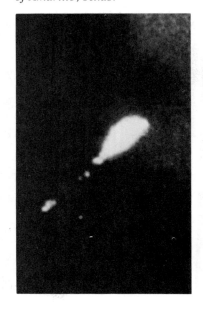

Photographer Richard Pipes captured this image of an unidentified object in the skies of Amarillo, Texas.

system for classifying UFO reports. His system has become the standard in the field. Hynek lists the following categories as ways to classify UFOs:

Nocturnal lights. Nocturnal, or nighttime, lights are the most common kinds of UFOs. Many nocturnal lights are simply lights in the sky, seen at some distance. Others appear as bright, glowing lights of various sizes and colors. In many cases, nocturnal lights seem to behave as if under intelligent control, performing unusual movements in the sky.

Daylight disks. Simply, these are UFOs seen in the daytime, at some distance. Witnesses usually describe daylight disks as solid, metallic objects, hovering above the ground or flying overhead. Sometimes, the disks seem to zoom off at fantastic speeds.

Radar-visual reports. Radar-visual reports occur when witnesses see UFOs and radar scopes detect the objects at the same time. In such cases, the radar contact seems to confirm the visual sighting.

Close encounters of the first kind (CE-I). Close encounters involve sightings of UFOs within five hundred feet. This is nearly the length of two football fields. In CE-I cases, UFOs do not interact with

A diagram illustrates how normal occurrences, such as clouds, stars, and meteors, are distorted by weather factors.

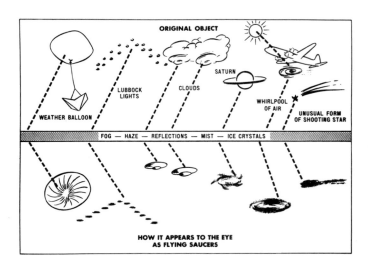

the surroundings or with witnesses. The UFOs simply appear in the sky or on the ground, within five hundred feet. There are hundreds of cases of this type.

Close encounters of the second kind (CE-II). CE-II cases involve UFOs that seemingly interact with their surroundings. The most common interactions are stalled automobiles and television interference. Other interactions include marks or burns on plants or on the ground and effects upon animals or humans.

Close encounters of the third kind (CE-III). CE-III cases involve witnesses seeing or claiming contact with creatures (most often humanoids or "ufonauts") associated with UFOs. Abduction reports are included in this category.

Something new to science?

With the publication of his book, Hynek was now convinced that UFOs represented something totally new to science. He boldly predicted that scientific knowledge would grow in one tremendous leap once scientists learned what UFOs are and how they got to earth. Little did Hynek or anyone else know that some startling events were about to happen. These events would make Hynek sound like a prophet. They would also deliver a series of harsh blows to the conclusions of the Condon Report.

Is this an alien or simply trick photography?

7

The Great Wave of 1973 and After: One Answer to the Condon Report

ON OCTOBER 11, 1973, Calvin Parker, nineteen years old, and Charles Hickson, forty-five, were fishing from a Pascagoula, Mississippi, pier at about 7:00 P.M. when they spotted a hazy blue object in the distance. They claimed the object approached them from across the water. The object, a bluish white, egg-shaped UFO about ten feet wide, came to within about thirty yards. It then stopped and hovered about three feet above the river bank.

Frozen in fear, the two men watched as a door opened "from nowhere," and three creatures emerged from the craft, floating toward them. Two of the creatures reached out with pincerlike arms and lifted the terrified Hickson into the air. Parker became hysterical, passed out, and did not wake up until the incident was over. He, too, was lifted while unconscious and taken inside the craft.

"The creatures were pale, ghostlike, about five feet high," said Hickson later. "They were sort of

An artist's drawing of spectators watching an approaching UFO.

"Well, here they come. ...You locked the keys inside, you do the talkin'."

light flesh-colored, or more pale grey, with crablike claws for hands and rounded feet." The creatures had "bulletlike" heads with no necks, slits for mouths, and wrinkled skin "like an elephant." For nose and ears, they had narrow, cone-shaped appendages sticking straight out. And strangest of all, they had no eyes.

Hickson was taken into a brightly lit room, where the two UFO creatures maneuvered him into a floating, horizontal position. Then a hovering eyelike device appeared and scanned Hickson, apparently doing some sort of physical examination. The creatures then left, leaving Hickson floating in the air for another twenty minutes or so. Hickson could not move a muscle during this time.

When the creatures returned, Hickson tried talking to them, but they ignored his questions. After this, Hickson and Parker were floated out of the craft and back to the ground.

"They carried me back outside and I floated down on my feet," said Hickson. "I was so weak-kneed, I think I fell over. The creatures didn't walk at all. Their legs stayed together and they floated. After I have thought about it, I believe they were more like robots. They acted like they had a specific thing to do, and they did it."

Parker was conscious now. He was weeping and praying as the strange craft rose straight up, emitted a buzzing sound, and disappeared into the distance.

Reporting to authorities

Fearing ridicule, the men at first did not report the incident. But thinking that the government might be interested in their story, they went later that night to the sheriff to report it.

At the station, Sheriff Fred Diamond and Capt. Glenn Ryder interviewed the two men, taping the conversations. To see if the story was a hoax, the of-

A drawing of Charles Hickson's encounter with a UFO.

ficers left Hickson and Parker alone for a while. They secretly kept the tape recorder running.

Parker, in a frantic voice, said, "I passed out. I expect I never passed out in my whole life."

Hickson responded, "I've never seen nothin' like this before in my life. You can't make people believe—"

Parker said, "I don't want to keep sittin' here. I want to see a doctor."

And Hickson said, "They better wake up and start believin'—they better start believin'."

Hickson also said, in a hysterical voice, "Why did this have to happen to me? I made it through the war—I've never been so scared!"

The conversation went on, and nothing was said that indicated a hoax. Sheriff Diamond later said,

Forty-five-year-old Charles Hickson claimed that he was abducted by alien creatures in 1973. Hickson reported that it was the most frightening experience of his life.

"First thing they wanted to do was take a lie detector test. Charlie, he was shook bad." He added that it is unusual to see a man of Hickson's age "break down and cry from excitement unless it's something fierce happened."

Hickson and Parker famous

Within days, the story was made public, and Hickson and Parker became famous nationwide. The Aerial Phenomena Research Organization (APRO) sent one of its scientific consultants, Dr. James Harder of the University of California at Berkeley, to interview the witnesses under regressive hypnosis. J. Allen Hynek went with Harder to do the investigation.

Harder concluded, "The experience they underwent was indeed a real one. A very strong feeling of terror is practically impossible to fake under hypnosis. . . . If this had been a hoax, they could have told the same story under hypnosis, but we would have lost the terror factor. There is no way they could have faked their terror." This terror became so great during hypnosis that several times the questioning had to be stopped.

Hynek agreed the story was genuine: "There's simply no question in my mind that these men have had a very real frightening experience, the physical nature of which I am not certain about. . . . They have had a fantastic experience and also I believe it should be taken in context with experiences that others have had elsewhere in this country and in the world."

Not all investigators agreed that the story happened as described, even though Hickson and Parker later passed a lie detector test. Phillip Klass, who believes the case is a hoax, discovered that this test was conducted by an inexperienced, unlicensed operator. Later when Hickson was asked to take a test conducted by an experienced, licensed operator, he declined.

Other reactions to the incident varied. *Newsweek* magazine was skeptical. It said, "Some [people] suspected there might well have been as much moonshine as stardust in the story." Ufologist John Keel said that Hickson and Parker suffered "a rather routine hallucination." But Hynek remained convinced, saying, "There was definitely something here that was not terrestrial."

The Pascagoula case occurred in the midst of a sensational wave of sightings. The wave spread across the United States and throughout parts of the world from 1973 through 1974 and even into the end of the decade. It was the greatest flap in UFO history and delivered a stunning blow to the conclusions of the Condon Report.

Nineteen-year-old Calvin Parker supports Hickson's account of a UFO abduction.

The Falkville creatures

UFO hysteria was running wild. On the evening of October 17, in Falkville, Alabama, police chief Jeff Greenhaw received a phone call about a UFO with flashing lights. The UFO had landed in a field near town. Driving to the site, he came across a humanoid creature clad in a silvery spacesuit with an antenna protruding from its helmet. Greenhaw stopped his patrol car, picked up his camera, and got out of the car as the creature walked toward him.

"The closer it got, the scareder I got," said Greenhaw. "I was shaking so, I could not move."

Greenhaw quickly flashed four photographs of the creature and said, "Howdy, stranger." The creature moved stiffly and made no sounds. Greenhaw stepped back to his car and turned on the blue, revolving light. The creature quickly turned and ran away down the dirt road. Greenhaw chased the creature in his car, but it got away. "He was running faster than any human I ever saw," said the police chief, adding, "I didn't believe in men from outer space, but I do now." The next day, Greenhaw received several calls from locals who had seen UFOs at the time of his encounter.

The Coyne helicopter incident

The night following Greenhaw's encounter was a clear, starry one. It was also a night that thirty-six-year-old Army captain Lawrence J. Coyne would never forget. Coyne was aboard a Bell UH-1H helicopter as copilot. He was flying at an altitude of 2,500 feet from Port Columbus, Ohio, to its home base at Cleveland Hopkins airport. En route, over Mansfield, Ohio, one of the crewmen spotted a red light on the horizon. The light seemed to keep pace with them, but after a while it began to close the gap between itself and the helicopter.

Fearing a collision, Coyne put the helicopter into a fast dive. At 1,700 feet, the object still raced straight toward them, and the terrorized crew braced for an impact. Suddenly, the object stopped about five hundred feet above the helicopter.

"It wasn't cruising, it was *stopped*," said the crew chief, Sgt. Robert Yanacsek. "For maybe ten to twelve seconds, just *stopped*."

The crewmen looked up to see a strange light bathing their helicopter. "It was shining brightly through the bubble canopy, turning everything inside green," Coyne said later. Through the light Coyne and his men saw a stunning sight. Above them was a metallic sixty-foot, cigar-shaped craft with a dome in the middle, a red light on the front end, and a green light on the back. Attempts to radio for help failed, even though the equipment seemed operational.

The crew felt a "bump" as the UFO suddenly zoomed off to the west. The green light changed to white as the object banked upward and disappeared.

An illustration of Army Capt. Lawrence J. Coyne occupying the helicopter that was accosted, Coyne claims, by a UFO.

Meanwhile, Coyne noticed the altimeter needle suddenly rising, even though all controls were set for a twenty-three degree dive. Without power, the helicopter rapidly rose to an altitude of 3,500 feet. The crewmen felt no stress or strain from the rise. Then, control of the helicopter returned, and radio contact with the ground resumed.

Later, some investigators speculated that the UFO itself had exerted some kind of control over the helicopter. Perhaps, they said, it had cut off the helicopter's communication and caused it to rise rapidly.

The incident was also seen from the ground. Two teenagers, both thirteen years old, saw the helicopter and the UFO positioned above it in the sky. They said the UFO looked "like a blimp" and was "as big as a school bus." They also saw the green light flare up.

"It was like rays coming down," said one of them. "The helicopter, the trees, the car—everything turned green."

Phillip Klass attributed the incident to "a fireball of the Orionid meteor shower." He said that such a meteor could have caused the green glow. He also said that the long, glowing trail of the meteor could have given the impression of a hovering object. The rapid rise, he said, was caused when Coyne pulled up on the controls without realizing it.

UFO investigators, however, stand by Coyne's account. They say that the duration of the incident, the apparent changes in course by the object, and the testimony of ground witnesses, all rule out Klass's argument.

The Lemon Grove incident

Following the Coyne incident, UFO reports continued to pour in. One unusual report took place at about 7:00 P.M. on the evening of November 16,

1973. Two eleven-year-olds, Richard Thiel and Danny Fleming of Lemon Grove, California, were playing in a field. They suddenly came across a strange, unfamiliar object, about eleven feet high and twenty feet in diameter. The boys approached it, and one of them banged the object with his flashlight. Abruptly, a domelike section on the top glowed a brilliant red, and the object rose three or four feet from the ground and began to rotate.

"Everything around turned red," said Fleming. "We immediately ran away."

As the object rose, it emitted a sound, much like a wailing siren. Green lights on the outside rim came on and began blinking on and off.

The boys experienced an unusual sensation as they ran away. "It felt to me like I was trying to run underwater," said Fleming. "Richard said he felt it was like trying to run in slow motion. We felt a tingling sensation all over . . . as though the hair on our arms was standing up."

Reaching Thiel's backyard, the boys looked back to see the object disappear into some clouds in the southwest. The time was now about 7:20.

An investigator examines the apparent landing tracks of a UFO.

Strange tracks

Examination of the landing area revealed three square-shaped holes, each about eight inches deep. Local UFO investigator Eric Herr reported, "The marks formed a triangle with seven-foot sides. There was dried grass and branches pressed into the holes." Dead grass in the area was lying in a counterclockwise pattern.

Nine residents in the area recalled having television interference from about 7:15 to 7:20 that evening, the same time the UFO took off. Additionally, a magnetometer (a device that detects shifts in magnetic fields) at Naval Oceans Systems Center's geomagnetic observatory registered a change at exactly 7:20 that evening.

With all the sightings pouring in, the American Institute of Public Opinion decided it was time to conduct a new Gallup poll to determine what the public thought about UFOs. The poll revealed that about 11 percent of Americans over the age of eighteen had at some time during their life seen a UFO (about fifteen million people). It also determined that sightings were reported by witnesses from virtually all types of jobs and professions.

Center for UFO studies formed

Hynek, meanwhile, fresh from investigating the Pascagoula case, was upset that there was no official place to report the sightings. He said, "It's scandalous that there's no agency to give or receive UFO information. People alarmed by these sightings deserve the security of knowing the government is looking into the matter."

Frustrated, Hynek decided to do something about it himself. Noting that "the study of UFOs has been grossly neglected but is eminently worthy of serious scientific study," he announced in late 1973 the formation of the Center for UFO Studies (CUFOS). This would be, he said, a "free association of scientists motivated by their common interest in the UFO problem." It would serve as a clearinghouse for the reporting of sightings and exchange of UFO information.

The Center would investigate cases, provide laboratory and technical analysis, and establish computer files for the storage of UFO information. In addition, it would publish technical reports, provide information to the public, and publish newsletters and scientific bulletins.

Police stations across the country were asked to take reports from the public and pass them on to the Center for investigation. The existing UFO

Dr. J. Allen Hynek appears at a research facility in Arizona.

groups—NICAP, APRO, and MUFON—were asked to share information with CUFOS. (The Center for UFO Studies is now known as the J. Allen Hynek Center for UFO Studies, renamed in honor of its founder, who died in April 1986.)

The Colusa UFOs

Over the next few years, the frantic pace of sightings slowed down but still continued at a higher than normal rate. There were many interesting cases but a few in particular stand out. One occurred in the early morning of September 10, 1976, in the rural community of Colusa, California. It was 12:45 A.M. when one household's power went out and mechanic Bill Pecha stepped outside to see what happened. Immediately, the hairs on his body stood up, as if charged with electricity. Above his barn hovered a domed, saucer-shaped object with a white, flat underside. Rows of lights rotated along the rim.

Pecha said, "It looked to me like it was 150 feet across and from 10 to 18 feet in height, shooting out beams of bluish light. It looked like a huge inverted cup and saucer with the outer rim spinning clockwise and an inner disk spinning counterclockwise."

Hooklike arms protruded from the edges, and cables dangled from the underside of the object. As it slowly moved over the adjoining field, the cables retracted completely, and the arms partially. A wide beam of light then projected toward the ground. The UFO moved over a neighbor's property and briefly lit the whole area.

In the distance, Pecha could see two more UFOs, shining blue beams of light down at power lines. Arching beams of light shot back up from the lines to the UFOs, as if energy were being tapped from the lines.

The main UFO then zoomed off toward the distant objects, only to return rapidly over the neigh-

bor's property. Further away, the smaller UFOs took off in opposite directions, and the power returned to Pecha's house. Pecha went inside for his wife and children, got in the car, and drove off at high speed. The main UFO seemed to follow the car as Pecha drove to the house of his friends. One of the friends came outside and saw the object before it finally disappeared.

Later, three other independent witnesses reported seeing an extremely bright light in the direction described by Pecha.

At about the same time as the sighting, there was a nine-minute power outage at the Pacific Gas & Electric substation in Victorville, California. This caused power losses in thousands of Northern California homes. Some suggested that the resulting power overload "caused static electricity to go into

An artist's portrayal of the UFO described by Bill Pecha after a 1976 sighting in Colusa, California.

the ground" and created a glow that was mistaken for a UFO.

Pecha laughed at this explanation. "It was big, it was real," he said. "It was terrifying—shafts of light seemingly coming at you, hovering over barns and houses, darting away, coming back, moving upward, then shooting back down close to the ground. I wasn't a believer in UFOs before, but I am now. I don't ever want to go through anything like this again."

The Iranian UFO chase

Nine days later, shortly after midnight on September 19, 1976, and halfway around the world, another unusual incident occurred. An Iranian Air Force F-4 Phantom jet was sent to intercept a UFO sighted over the city of Tehran. Witnesses said the object flashed extremely bright strobelike lights in alternating colors of blue, green, red, and orange. As the jet pursued the object northward for about forty miles, the jet's communications equipment and instrumentation went out. The jet then turned back, and all communications and instrumentation returned to working order.

At 1:40 A.M., a second F-4 was sent out. It chased the UFO at a distance of about thirty miles. All of a sudden, another, smaller bright UFO came out of the original one. It headed straight for the pursuing jet. The pilot tried to fire a missile, but his weapons control panel would not function and his communications quit working.

Frightened, the pilot put his jet into a dive to avoid possible attack. The smaller UFO then circled behind and returned to the mother ship. Seconds later, another smaller craft emerged from the other side of the mother ship. It dove toward the ground, shining a bright light over a 1 1/2-mile area, and landed. As the pilot cruised lower to take a look, the

UFO took off and reentered the mother ship, which then zoomed away.

The F-4 returned to the airport. Just as it was landing, the pilot, radar operator, and ground controllers all witnessed another astonishing sight. They saw a huge cylindrical UFO with lights on the ends and a flashing light in the middle pass overhead.

Secret reports

Later, Maj. Roland B. Evans, an analyst for the U.S. Defense Intelligence Agency, wrote of this case, "An outstanding report. This case is a classic which meets all the criteria necessary for a valid study of a UFO phenomenon." His report was kept secret until an organization called Citizens Against UFO Secrecy (CAUS) went to court and sought its release under the Freedom of Information and Privacy Act. (This legislation was enacted by Congress as a way for ordinary citizens to obtain unreasonably withheld government information.)

The time period between the mid-1970s and the end of that decade marked a turning point. One era in UFO history ended, and a new one began. To ufologists, the great wave of 1973 and its aftermath had refuted the results of the Condon Report. Now it was time to move on.

Continued sightings of UFOs, despite their strangeness, were failing to provide any new information. A new kind of report, however, was surfacing in ever greater numbers. These reports told of bizarre and frightening abductions by space creatures. Investigators were growing alarmed and turned their attention to this new challenge before it got out of hand. The entire UFO field of investigation was about to be swept into the most incredible and startling time of its history.

8

The Abduction Era: Frightening Creatures, Kidnappings, and Medical Experiments

A picture of a man getting zapped with a beam of light from an approaching UFO.

IT WAS ABOUT 1:15 A.M. on August 13, 1975, that the life of Air Force Sergeant Charles L. Moody was changed forever. Moody's story follows: He was in the desert near Alamogordo, New Mexico. He was watching a meteor shower when he saw a strange, glowing, metallic disk descending in wobbly fashion toward him. It emitted a high-pitched droning sound. Moody jumped back into his car, but it would not start. Petrified, he watched as the object came to a stop about seventy-five feet away. The droning stopped, and a numbness spread through his body.

Then everything went blank, and the next thing he knew, he was watching the object lift off into the sky. He started the car and drove home, arriving there at 3:00 A.M. He then realized he could not account for about an hour and a half of his time.

Within the next few days, Moody experienced pains in his back and developed rashes on his body. An examination revealed a small puncture wound over his spine. A doctor suggested that Moody use self-hypnosis techniques to discover what happened during the missing time.

Slowly, the memory returned. Moody recalled seeing the UFO, becoming numb, and watching two creatures approach him. "These beings did not walk, they glided," he said. "They put their hands on the car and I guess they were trying to figure out how to get the door open." Moody opened the door into one of the creatures and struck out at the other.

"The next thing I knew I was completely and totally paralyzed," he added.

The creatures made Moody become unconscious. They took him aboard the craft, where he awoke on a slab, still paralyzed.

Beside Moody stood two humanoids, each about six feet tall with large bald heads, small ears and nose, thin lips, large round eyes, and grey-white skin. Both wore black, skintight uniforms. Next to them stood a third humanoid, the leader. He was similar except that he was about five feet tall and was wearing a silvery suit.

The leader spoke to Moody by projecting thoughts into his mind. He asked Moody if he would behave. When Moody indicated he would, the leader placed a rodlike device to his back, and the paralysis ended. The aliens then took Moody on a tour of the craft and told him that their mother ship was stationed in high earth orbit. They said that he would have no memory of his abduction for about two weeks. They also said that they would not come back for about another twenty years.

The leader put his hands on the sides of Moody's head, and he fell unconscious again. The next thing Moody knew, he was sitting in his car watching the UFO fly away.

Moody was treated at an army hospital, where he was told he had been exposed to radiation. Mysteriously, the records of his treatment disappeared. Doctors and nurses remembered seeing him but could not account for the missing records.

A model of an alien creature, constructed by Betty Ann Luca, who claims to have encountered a similar creature in 1967.

The Travis Walton affair

Another, much more publicized case occurred on November 5, 1975, at about 6:15 P.M. Six young woodcutters and their employer drove a pickup truck down a mountainside about fifteen miles from the small town of Heber, Arizona. Travis Walton, twenty-two years old, was riding on the passenger side when one of the men spotted a glowing object hovering about fifteen feet above the ground, in a clearing. The driver stopped, and Walton leaped out to take a closer look. The object, which looked like two shallow bowls placed rim to rim, emitted a beeping sound.

Suddenly, a blue-green beam of light shot down from the bottom of the object. It struck Walton in the head and chest, lifted him into the air, and tossed him back down.

"I felt kind of an electric shock throughout my whole body," said Walton, "and that's all I can remember."

Walton's friends, fearing for their lives, raced off in the truck. As they drove away, they looked back to see a light taking off into the northeast.

The men returned to the clearing with flashlights and searched the area for fifteen minutes. They could find no sign of Walton. After debating what to

"Yes, yes, already, Warren! . . . There *is* film in the camera!"

do, they decided to report their experience to the sheriff in Heber. The story soon hit the press wires, and hundreds of reporters flocked to Arizona. Meanwhile, authorities searched for the missing woodcutter.

When Walton did not show up anywhere over the next few days, some people suspected foul play. On November 10, the men who had been with Walton took lie detector tests to see if they had a part in Walton's disappearance. They were also tested to see if they had really seen the UFO. They passed the tests.

A desperate call for help

That very evening, Walton's sister in Snowflake, Arizona, received a desperate phone call. It was Walton, calling from a phone booth in Heber. He seemed disoriented and was in much pain.

Walton's brother Duane raced to Heber, where he found Walton slumped in a phone booth, about twelve miles from the spot where he first disappeared. Duane helped him into his truck. Groggy but able to talk, Walton babbled about being taken aboard a UFO by "awful" creatures who "kept looking" at him with "horrible eyes."

As they headed home toward Snowflake, Walton was surprised at the growth of beard on his face. He wondered how it could have grown so much after being unconscious for only "a couple of hours." After all, he said, he could remember only "about an hour or an hour and a half inside that thing." Walton could hardly believe it when told he had been missing for five days.

Walton was given a battery of medical, psychological, and lie detector tests. Included in these tests was a regressive hypnosis session conducted by Dr. James Harder, who was sent in by APRO as a part of its hands-on investigation. This session did not reveal anything new, but it convinced Harder that in Walton's mind, the story was real.

According to Walton, after his abduction, he "woke" to find himself on a table in a hospital-like room, filled with damp, muggy air. Around him stood three creatures with large, bald, domed heads and pale, "marshmallowish" skin. They also had brown eyes the size of quarters.

Terrified, Walton jumped up and tried to attack his captors. They quickly left the room, and Walton, in a panic, fled. He ran to an open door and went into a strange room where he saw a transparent wall displaying stars. In the middle of the room stood a chair with buttons. Walton pressed one of the buttons and the stars began to move.

Suddenly, Walton noticed a man, human in appearance, standing in the doorway, wearing a hel-

Travis Walton described his captors as bald and pale. Here, an artist depicts Walton defending himself against the creatures.

met. The man led Walton from the craft and into a large enclosed area where there were several other disk-shaped craft and other humans. They placed a device similar to an oxygen mask over Walton's face, and he passed out. He awoke to find himself lying on a road. Overhead, he saw the disk-shaped UFO rising, its doors closing. He watched as the object disappeared from sight. In a confused mental state, Walton made his way to the phone booth in Heber.

Controversy surrounded this case from the start. Charges and counter charges flew as APRO and other UFO groups fought for exclusive control of the case. Lie detector tests given to Walton were inconclusive, and in the end ufologists were left with yet another strange encounter to ponder for years to come.

Before passing out, Walton claims he saw several human-looking creatures aboard the space ship.

One of the most astounding abduction cases is that of "Kathie Davis" (a pseudonym for the real person). Kathie's story is told in the book *Intruders: The Incredible Visitations at Copley Woods*, by abduction ufologist Budd Hopkins.

Ufologists consider the case important not only for its content but for its physical evidence. This evidence was found in the form of a circular, eight-foot UFO landing site of dead grass in Kathie's backyard.

In 1983, Kathie wrote to Hopkins, whose earlier book, *Missing Time: A Documented Study of UFO Abductions*, she had read. In her letter she described a disturbing series of dreams, beginning in 1978, in which she was abducted by UFO beings. Hopkins met Kathie and hypnotized her over a period of time. He became convinced that Kathie's abduction dreams were based on real events.

Under hypnosis, Kathie told a horrifying story. She revealed that she was made pregnant by a ufonaut, only to see the unborn fetus removed from her body by the ufonauts. The unborn was then transplanted to the body of an extraterrestrial female for continued growth and eventual birth. Later, the ufonauts let Kathie meet this hybrid offspring face-to-face, a little girl who was half earthling and half extraterrestrial.

This case, together with others studied by Hopkins, forced him to come to an alarming conclusion. He was now convinced that extraterrestrials were conducting interbreeding experiments on thousands of people worldwide. This was a frightening prospect, if true.

The Whitley Strieber case

In February 1986, another person wrote to Hopkins about a disturbing experience that reportedly happened in December 1985. The correspondent was Whitley Strieber, a well-known author of horror stories. Strieber's only prior knowledge about UFOs reportedly came from reading a few UFO books.

After talking to Strieber, Hopkins suggested that he see a psychotherapist, a person who treats mental problems. Strieber underwent four regressive hypnosis sessions with Dr. Ronald F. Klein, director of research at the New York State Psychiatric Institute.

Strieber's story is as follows. On the night of December 26, 1985, he awoke to a strange "whooshing" sound coming from the living room downstairs in his woodlands cabin. He got up to see a "compact figure" wearing a "gray-tan body suit" entering his room. According to Strieber, it had "two dark eyeholes and a round smooth mouth hole."

Then a "blackness" overcame Strieber for an unknown period of time. His next conscious memory was that of being "in motion" and finding himself in the woods outside his cabin.

Strieber could remember seeing four ufonauts in all: a small, robotlike creature; a pug-nose creature wearing blue coveralls; a delicate slender creature with "mesmerizing black slanting eyes"; and a smaller being with black, buttonlike eyes.

Strange, frightening experiences

Under hypnosis by Klein, Strieber told of additional experiences. On one occasion, a ufonaut touched Strieber's head with a wandlike device. The device planted visual images of a nuclear war in his mind. On another occasion, a female ufonaut warned Strieber that the space aliens planned to stick a thin needle into his brain as part of an operation. On yet another occasion, dwarflike humanoids visited him in his room.

Because Strieber was a well-known author,

An artist's version of three ufonauts.

people paid attention to his story. His books *Communion* and *Transformation*, discussing his UFO experiences, became best-sellers.

Hypnotist thinks Strieber case a hoax

The man who hypnotized Strieber does not believe Strieber was really abducted by ufonauts. In a letter to Strieber, Klein said that these manifestations could be the result of an "abnormality in the temporal lobe" of the brain. This is a medical condition that could explain many of Strieber's experiences. A medical test, however, showed that Strieber did not have this abnormality.

The possible meanings of these and many other abduction reports are tremendous, if they are indeed taking place as described. Ufologist David Webb says, "The abduction reports are important, because the chance of misidentification is small. It's not a light in the sky. People are either hoaxing, or there's some psychological disorder, or the case is real. Those are the basic options."

Questions about regressive hypnosis

But are these cases happening as described? Scientists such as James Harder and Leo Sprinkle, and investigators such as Budd Hopkins, have used regressive hypnosis as the primary means of uncovering these bizarre and frightening stories. Most psychiatrists, however, warn that there are problems in using this method as the only source of evidence. The biggest problem, they say, is that the subconscious mind often "remembers" dreams as "real" experiences. This part of the mind often cannot tell the difference between dreams and real memories.

UFO investigator Joseph Santangelo listens to a hypnotized patient recall her abduction by a UFO.

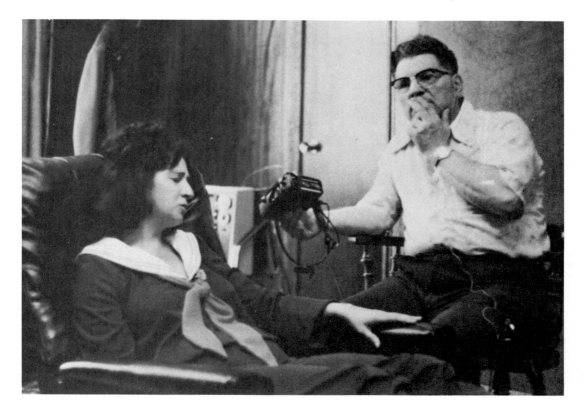

Another problem is that answers given under regressive hypnosis can sometimes be based on information gained from sources that are not first-hand encounters. Reading books or viewing movies, for instance, can influence answers given by the subject. Certain questions and comments made by the hypnotist can also shape a subject's response. In other words, details can be picked up and "planted" into the mind as pseudo, or false, memories and recalled under hypnosis as real ones.

Are UFO abductions fantasies?

An interesting experiment was conducted in 1977 to test this concept. Results of the experiment suggest that people who have never really experienced abductions can, under hypnosis, create such experiences in their minds.

Two UFO researchers selected eight people who, under hypnosis, were first told to imagine or visualize being taken aboard a UFO. They were also told to imagine that they were given physical examinations and then released. No other details were provided. They were then asked, while still hypnotized, to describe their "experiences." Each of the eight did so. They even added details, including descriptions of space aliens and their UFOs, that were never suggested to them by the hypnotist.

The resulting stories were compared to four actual abduction accounts, including the case of Betty and Barney Hill. Surprisingly, the stories were nearly identical.

The experiment showed that the subconscious mind, while under hypnosis, is capable of inventing colorful details to describe events that may never have happened. It seemed to cast doubt on the reliability of regressive hypnosis as a tool for ufologists.

Indeed, according to experts, the frustrating thing about regressive hypnosis is that it can reveal details of events that *did* happen, or it can reveal details of events that *did not* happen. Mental health professionals can usually determine if statements are based on dreams, planted memories, or real experiences. Untrained investigators, however, might not be able to do this.

These factors serve to confuse the information received through regressive hypnosis. Are the abduction stories based on real events or just dreams and planted memories? Researchers are still looking for the answers.

9

Investigating UFOs: Using Reason to Solve the Mystery

UFOLOGISTS HAVE TRIED for a long time to prove that UFOs represent some kind of strange and unusual phenomena. At the same time, military and government officials, as well as some scientists, have tried to identify UFOs as natural events or human-made objects. Both sides, in essence, have continually searched for a good hypothesis—a proposed explanation for an observed event or behavior—to account for UFOs.

After many years of research, ufologists and scientists alike have developed many hypotheses. These fall into two categories: unconventional and conventional. Unconventional hypotheses treat UFOs as strange or unusual objects, usually connected to some form of intelligence. Conventional hypotheses attribute UFOs to natural or human-made phenomena, neither of which is the result of an alien intelligence.

The Extraterrestrial Hypothesis maintains that

A series of UFOs over South Yorkshire in England was photographed by Stephen Pratt on March 28, 1966.

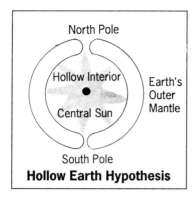

North Pole

Hollow Interior

Central Sun

Earth's Outer Mantle

South Pole

Hollow Earth Hypothesis

This diagram shows one version of the hollow earth theory. The interior of the earth is supposed to be inhabited by citizens of Atlantis or aliens using the area as a base camp for trips to the surface of the earth.

UFOs are spacecraft piloted by beings from other planets. This explanation assumes that many civilizations exist throughout the galaxy. It also assumes that some of these civilizations have found efficient ways to travel the long distances between star systems. Supporters of this explanation cite the many reports of spacecraftlike landings, humanoid sightings, and abductions as evidence.

Demonic UFOs

The Demonic Forces Hypothesis claims that UFOs represent demons coming to earth in preparation for the final battle between good and evil. It is closely tied to biblical prophecies. Accordingly, creatures from the demonic UFOs will use all kinds of trickery to fool humanity into thinking they are friendly.

The Hollow Earth Hypothesis is a bizarre explanation proposing that the earth is hollow and that UFOs come from civilizations existing inside the earth. The UFOs reportedly enter and exit the hollow earth from openings at the north and south poles. Scientific evidence strongly refutes this explanation.

The Space Animals Hypothesis proposes that some UFOs are actually living creatures, space animals that live in the atmosphere. One variation of this explanation claims that these creatures are amoeba-like, and made of a strange material that is invisible most of the time.

The Space Brothers Hypothesis claims that UFOs represent kindly, mystical beings, or space brothers from other worlds. A contactee usually claims repeated contact with the space brothers, passing along their messages to the rest of humanity. These messages usually offer to save the world from disease, pollution, and nuclear war.

The Time Machines Hypothesis explains that

UFOs are time machines traveling here from our own future. The UFO occupants, even though physically different from us, are thought to be advanced versions of ourselves.

The Underwater Civilizations Hypothesis is based on observations of UFOs entering and leaving bodies of water. It states that UFO intelligences have established secret bases along the ocean floors to conceal their activities.

The Ultraterrestrial Hypothesis is an increasingly popular explanation that claims UFOs come from other dimensions, worlds parallel to our own. The UFOs serve as vehicles for crossing from one dimension to another.

Conventional explanations

The Hallucinations/Dreams Hypothesis proposes that *some* UFO reports are hallucinations, or imagined happenings that seem real to the observer. Hallucinations are most likely to occur to people who have emotional or mental problems. Under certain circumstances, such people might *believe* they see something when really nothing is there. Others may see UFOs or experience abductions in their dreams. Later, under regressive hypnosis, the stories emerge as real experiences.

The Hoaxes Hypothesis says that some UFO reports are the result of deliberate deception. Indeed, skeptical investigators and enthusiasts alike acknowledge that frauds and hoaxes make up an uncertain portion of UFO cases. Investigators recognize that photographs especially tend to be faked. However, there are no reliable statistics, because it is impossible to determine how many of the 5 to 10 percent of "unexplained" cases could really be hoaxes.

The Natural/Man-made Phenomena Hypothesis claims most UFOs are natural or human-made. For

George Adamski claims to have visited other planets and to have made trips to outer space.

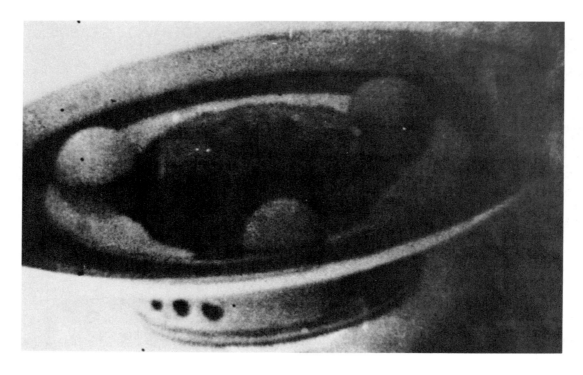

Can this photograph of a mysterious object be man-made?

example, natural objects such as birds, clouds, stars, planets, as well as tricks of the atmosphere are frequently reported as UFOs. Additionally, human-made objects such as aircraft and aircraft lights, balloons, blimps, and searchlight reflections are also reported as UFOs. Skeptics believe that most UFO reports can be explained this way. Ufologists try to eliminate these explanations in an effort to create a reliable information base.

The Secret Weapons Hypothesis was especially popular in the early 1950s. It proposes that some reported UFOs are secret weapons being tested by the U.S. government or foreign military powers. Few people now support this explanation.

The Null Hypothesis is an explanation for UFOs that was refined by skeptical investigator Robert Sheaffer. It means, simply, that UFOs, as spaceships from other worlds, do not exist. This explanation, says Sheaffer, is the only one that scientifically accounts for all aspects of the UFO riddle. Sheaffer charges that verifiable evidence for UFOs as space-ships is missing because these spacecraft exist only in the imaginations of the observers. The null hypothesis, he says, is the only valid explanation. This is because it acknowledges known facts and does not rely on new scientific laws or unscientific concepts of nature.

Unproven hypotheses

To this point, researchers have been unable to verify any of the explanations. The theories are difficult to prove because UFOs pose special problems. The sightings occur unexpectedly and last for only a short time. Investigators cannot usually get to

Joseph Simonton holds up an object he says was given to him by the occupant of a flying saucer that landed on his chicken farm in 1961.

the site until the incident is over. Witnesses usually have little more than a story to tell as evidence. And that is precisely why there is so much controversy about UFOs.

Some scientists do not accept UFOs at all because to them, stories alone do not prove anything. They ask for something more substantial, such as hard physical evidence that can be picked up and analyzed in a laboratory. Marks on the ground, soil samples, and photographs are a step in the right direction. But, they say, these things are not enough to establish the nature and origin of UFOs.

What scientists look for

Just what kinds of evidence would it take to convince most scientists UFOs are real? The following list gives some examples of evidence that could es-

A group of students demonstrate how they deliberately launched plastic bags filled with candles and hot air. These bags deceived unsuspecting observers, who thought they had seen a UFO.

"Listen! Just follow our distress beacon and send some help! . . . We're in quadrant 57 of the Milky Way – on a planet called 'Bob's Shoeworld.'"

tablish the origin and identity of UFOs:

1) Materials, received from the ufonauts, that are beyond the manufacturing capabilities of modern science and industry.

2) Specimens from living creatures (skin cells, hair, etc.) showing a biological or chemical structure different from our own.

3) Advanced scientific information, given by the space beings, that could be confirmed by our own scientists.

4) Face-to-face meetings between the ufonauts and leaders of government, science, and the military.

In 1950, nineteen-year-old Arthur Sanger sets loose his jet-propelled model flying saucer.

Investigating UFOs requires special care. Weeding out the natural explanations and hoaxes is the primary task of the investigator, and it is a difficult one.

Using the scientific method

Someday you may see a UFO, or you may question someone who did. If you become involved in any way, you will want to do things in a scientific manner. The scientific method is a time-tested procedure used throughout the world for investigations. It allows you to be organized and conduct yourself in a systematic manner. It also allows you to be skeptical about your work.

How should *you* use this method?

First, start with an open mind. Do not decide ahead of time what UFOs are. Let your review of the facts determine that. Having an open mind does not mean that you should accept anything and everything as evidence. You must set certain standards to make sure the information gathered is accurate and reliable. Accepting false or distorted information will result in faulty conclusions.

Here are the steps to take:

Step 1. *Make observations.* Keep accurate records of everything you see and find.

Step 2. *Try to explain the observations.* What happened during your observations? What are the possible explanations? Which seems best? We call this first, untested explanation a hypothesis, a *possible* explanation.

Step 3. *Test your explanation.* Try creating an experiment or a study to see if your hypothesis is good. Because there is seldom anything to take into a laboratory for study, you must adjust this step somewhat for UFOs. For instance, you can evaluate the reliability of the witnesses and their stories. Does the witness usually tell the truth, or is he or she known for stretching the truth? Does the witnes's story make sense, or can you find inconsistencies in it? Was there more than one witness to the sighting? If so, compare the stories offered by the witnesses to see if they are the same. When questioning the witnesses, be careful not to ask leading questions. For example, ask what shape the UFO was instead of asking whether the UFO was round or oval. This method helps get a more accurate description of the UFO.

Step 4. *Reach a conclusion.* Look at the results of your experiment or investigation. Do they support your hypothesis? Sometimes the results are uncertain. If so, try taking a new approach or fine-tuning your original investigation.

Step 5. *Repeat the test.* Go through your investigation again to see if the results are the same.

Step 6. *Report the results.* Once you are satisfied, report your findings. The process of reporting is called peer review. You might submit your findings to your science teacher or send a report to either the J. Allen Hynek Center for UFO Studies or to the Mutual UFO Network. Both groups usually respond to people who report UFO sightings. This step lets others check your work for errors and eliminate results that might be based on faulty research.

Scientific observations controversial

Some ufologists carefully follow scientific procedures. Others do not. This is yet another reason the field remains so controversial today. Most of the debates about UFOs concern the quality of the investigations and the reliability of the conclusions. They usually do not question the fact that the witnesses originally saw something.

As you start your exploration of the UFO challenge, follow the steps. Use organized procedures in questioning people. Keep records and look for the

Photograph of a UFO hovering over Passaic, New Jersey in August of 1952.

four kinds of evidence that scientists would accept. And evaluate the work of other investigators to see if *they* are following the steps. After all, a great mystery remains, and it is possible that the case you explore will be the big one the world has been waiting for.

Glossary

abductee: A person who claims to have been, or believes that he has been, kidnapped by UFO creatures.

APRO: The Aerial Phenomena Research Organization. APRO was organized in 1952 by Jim and Coral Lorenzen to investigate UFOs. Once the world's largest UFO organization, the group disbanded after the death of its founders.

ball lightning: A glowing ball of light, also known as "corona discharge" or St. Elmo's fire. It is occasionally seen traveling along power lines or hovering around the masts of ships during electrical storms.

CAUS: The Citizens Against UFO Secrecy. Members of this organization believe that various military and government agencies have covered up important facts about UFOs discovered during investigations.

contactee: A person who claims personal and repeated contact with alien intelligences, most often wise, kindly space brothers. The contactee usually presents himself as a messenger between the space brothers and humanity.

CUFOS: The Center for UFO Studies, now known as the J. Allen Hynek Center for UFO Studies. This organization collects reports, investigates sightings, and stores UFO information in computer files. It also publishes papers and reports for distribution to scientists, researchers, and the public.

extraterrestrial: Outside the earth or its atmosphere. In ufology, it especially refers to something, or someone, from outer space or another planet.

flap: A series, or wave, of UFO sightings.

flying saucer: An outdated term for UFO. Over the years, ufologists have stopped using this term because it assumes that UFOs are saucer-shaped spaceships. (Many UFOs do not fit this description.)

galaxy: A large group of stars held together by gravity.

humanoid: A humanlike occupant of a UFO.

hypothesis: A proposed explanation for observed events or behaviors.

IFO: Identified flying object. A UFO that is identified following investigation. For example, a UFO that is identified as a weather balloon becomes an IFO.

light-year: The distance light travels in one year, at the speed of 186,000 miles per second. This distance is 5,878,000,000,000 miles, or nearly 6 trillion miles.

mother ship: A huge UFO, sometimes cigar-shaped, that holds smaller UFOs.

MUFON: The Mutual UFO Network. MUFON was founded in 1969 as the Midwest UFO Network. Later, the organization expanded nationally and adopted its present name. The organization conducts field investigations and publishes a newsletter. It also conducts seminars and sponsors a yearly national conference on UFOs. It is now the largest UFO organization in the world.

NICAP: The National Investigations Committee on Aerial Phenomena. NICAP was founded in 1956 by Maj. Donald E. Keyhoe. The organization collected reports and published booklets and newsletters. It successfully lobbied for congressional hearings on UFOs. The organization, once the most influential in the country, is no longer active.

regressive hypnosis: A hypnosis technique for obtaining information that may be "hidden" in the subconscious parts of the mind. It helps subjects recall things that may have happened or things the mind believes have happened.

theory: A comprehensive explanation of an event or behavior. It is usually developed from a series of hypotheses that have been tested.

UFO: Unidentified flying object. Something that is seen in the air or on the ground and that, after considerable investigation, remains unidentified.

ufologist: One who studies, researches, or investigates UFO reports, usually in support of one of the unconventional explanations.

ufology: The study of UFO reports.

ufonaut: An occupant of a flying saucer or UFO.

ultraterrestrial: "Otherworldly"; usually referring to other dimensions or parallel worlds.

Organizations to Contact

Arcturus Book Service
P.O. Box 831383
Stone Mountain, GA 30083-0023

International UFO Reporter
(Center for UFO Studies publication)
1511 Greenleaf St.
Evanston, IL 60202

The J. Allen Hynek Center for UFO Studies
2457 W. Peterson Ave.
Chicago, IL 60659

Mutual UFO Network/MUFON UFO Journal
103 Oldtowne Road
Seguin, TX 78155

The UFO Archives
P.O. Box 264
Marion, IA 52302

UFO Newsclipping Service
Route 1, Box 220
Plumerville, AR 72127

William L. Moore Publications & Research
4219 W. Olive St., Suite 247
Burbank, CA 91505

Suggestions for Further Reading

Rhoda Blumberg, *UFO*. New York: Franklin Watts, 1977.

Daniel Cohen, *Creatures from UFOs*. New York: Dodd, Mead, 1978.

Daniel Cohen, *The Great Airship Mystery*. New York: Dodd, Mead, 1981.

Daniel Cohen, *The World of UFOs*. New York: J.B. Lippincott, 1978.

Rita Golden Gelman and Marcia Seligson, *UFO Encounters*. New York: Scholastic Book Service, 1978.

Susan Harris, *UFOs*. New York: Franklin Watts, 1980.

David C. Knight, *Those Mysterious UFOs: The Story of Unidentified Flying Objects*. New York: Parents Magazine Press, 1975.

David C. Knight, *UFOs: A Pictorial History from Antiquity to the Present*. New York: McGraw-Hill, 1979.

Sherman J. Larsen, *Close Encounters: A Factual Report on UFOs*. Milwaukee: Raintree, 1978.

Ann M. and Harry F. Mayer, *Who's Out There? UFO Encounters*. New York: Julian Messner, 1979.

Richard Rasmussen, *The UFO Literature: A Comprehensive Annotated Bibliography of Works in English*. Jefferson, North Carolina: McFarland, 1985.

Bob Rickard, *UFOs*. New York: Gloucester Press, 1979.

Janet Riehecky, *UFOs*. Chicago: The Child's World/Children's Press, 1989.

Jonathan Rutland, *UFOs*. New York: Random House, 1987.

Peter Ryan and Ludek Pesek, *UFOs and Other Worlds*. Harmondsworth, England: Puffin Books/Penguin Books, 1975.

Index

Picture Credits

Cover Illustration: FAB Artists, Minneapolis, MN.

AP/Wide World Photos, 9, 13, 15, 18, 20, 27, 28, 31, 32, 38, 40, 58, 79, 91, 99, 113, 115
THE FAR SIDE ©1988 Universal Press Syndicate. Reprinted with permission. All rights reserved, 64, 117
THE FAR SIDE cartoons by Gary Larson are reproduced by permission of Chronicle Features, San Francisco, CA 84, 100
Fortean Picture Library, 110, 119
Courtesy Raymond Fowler, 107
Reprinted from *The Edge of Reality* by J. Allen Hynek, Regnery, © 1975, 51
J. Allen Hynek Center for UFO Studies, 10, 14, 22, 23, 25, 29, 34, 35, 36, 46, 48, 50, 56, 60, 61, 66, 67, 72, 73, 76, 77, 78, 81, 85, 86, 87, 88, 93, 96, 102, 103, 114
ICUFON Archives, 24
From *The Interrupted Journey* by John G. Fuller. New York: Dial Books, 1966, 53

Amy Johnson, 106
From the book *LIGHT YEARS*. Copyright © 1987 by Gary Kinder and Intercep. Reproduced here by permission of the Atlantic Monthly Press, 6, 90
Mary Evans Picture Library, 8, 12, 30, 37, 82
Hannah McRoberts/Fortean Picture Library, 70
Minneapolis Public Library Picture Collection, 54
Oliphant, copyright © 1967 Universal Press Syndicate. Reprinted with permission. All rights reserved, 75
The "Bizarre" cartoon by Dan Piraro is reprinted by permission of Chronicle Features, San Francisco, CA, 98
Sky & Telegraph photograph by J. Kelly Beatty, 68
Smithsonian Institution, 17
UPI Bettmann Newsphotos, 26, 33, 43, 52, 63, 80, 116, 118

Every effort has been made to trace owners of copyright material.

About the Author

Richard Michael Rasmussen is a professional writer and a social service worker with the county of San Diego. Mr. Rasmussen holds an AA degree in social science from Grossmont College and a certificate in technical writing. While *The UFO Challenge* is his first book for Lucent Books, Mr. Rasmussen has written several others, including *The UFO Literature,* published by McFarland and Company, and *The Kid's Enclyclopedia of Things to Make and Do* published by Toys 'n' Things Press. As a member of the national Society of Children's Book Writers, Mr. Rasmussen is very interested in encouraging young people to write. He presently gives talks at elementary and junior high schools in hopes of inspiring young people to become professional writers.